T0129205

SUPER SNACKS

100 Favorite Snacks from Five Continents

INDERJEET RISHI

Trafford rev. 10/10/2012

 www.trafford.com

North America & international
toll-free: 1 888 232 4444 (USA & Canada)
phone: 250 383 6864 ♦ fax: 812 355 4082

CONTENTS

To my loving husband Tilak Rishi
with love, devotion and gratitude

INTRODUCTION

Super Snacks is compiled from my series of blog-posts already published in inderjeetrishi.blogspot.com and sulekha.com under the tag World-Bites, a collection of recipes for bite-size dishes and appetizers from around the world. Every culture in the world has developed a certain taste and preference for the type of food its people consume. The factors that influence these preferences include their natural resources, climate, economic condition and cultural beliefs. If you compare Asian food culture to the culture of nations from the West, there is a considerable difference between the types of food consumed, preference toward flavors, and the most consumed common food in the area: their food staple. This book is about the most favorite food snacks in the 5 inhabited continents—the Americas, Europe, Africa, Asia and Australia.

Those pressed for time will find World-bites simple yet impressive preparations which would come handy any time of the day as in—between—the meals snacks or some even as substitutes for the main meals. Even better, a number of nearly 100 recipes require little prep time and assume basic know-how on the part of the home chef. Some recipes may involve many ingredients which are not always the easiest to find and are time consuming, the result however, is so much worth it. Super Snacks is for whoever loves cooking and understands the dedication that good food takes, even when it is not a full meal. There is a recipe for every taste or international food preference for which I profusely thank my friends from far and near who helped me with their valued input to make Super Snacks truly representative of different regions in the world. Still, to make it more inclusive of food from different cultures and countries, I thank readers of my blogs for contributing recipes from their region through comments, which I have incorporated in the book to make Super Snacks more meaningful and enjoyable for all. Indeed, I will be ever thankful for their help.

Inderjeet Rishi

The Continent of the Americas

North American cuisine is a term used for foods native to or popular in countries of North America, as with Canadian cuisine, Cuisine of the United States, and Cuisine of Mexico. It has influences from many international cuisines, including Native American cuisine and European cuisine. Mexican cuisine is known for its intense and varied flavors, colorful decoration, and variety of spices. Mexican culture and food is one of the richest in the world, both with respect to diverse and appealing tastes and textures; and in terms of proteins, vitamins, and minerals. Most of today's Mexican cuisine is based on pre-Hispanic traditions, including the Aztecs, Maya, and the Indigenous peoples of Mexico combined with culinary trends introduced by Spanish colonists. Mexican cuisine varies by region, because of local climate and geography and ethnic differences among the indigenous inhabitants and because these different populations were influenced by the Spaniards in varying degrees.

Caribbean cuisine is a fusion of African, Dutch, Amerindian, French, Indian, and Spanish cuisine. These traditions were brought from the many homelands of this region's population. In addition, the population has created from this vast wealth of tradition many styles that are unique to the region. Seafood is one of the most common cuisine types in the islands, though this is certainly due in part to their location. Each island will likely have its own specialty. Some prepare lobster, while others prefer certain types of fish. For example, the island of Barbados is known for its "flying fish." Another Caribbean mainstay is rice, but you'll find the rice on each island may be a little different. Some season their rice, or add peas and other touches—like coconut. Sometimes the rice is yellow, but other times it is part of a dish. Though it comes in many forms, it is a common side dish throughout the region.

Latin American Cuisine refers to typical foods, beverages, and cooking styles common to many of the countries and cultures in Latin America. Latin America is a highly diverse area of land that holds various cuisines that vary from nation to nation. Some items typical of Latin American cuisine include maize-based dishes (tortillas, tamales, pupusas) and various salsas and other condiments (guacamole, pico de gallo, mole, chimichurri, and pebre). These spices are generally what give the Latin American cuisines a distinct flavor; yet, each country of Latin America tends to use a different spice and those that share spices tend to use them at different quantities. Thus, this leads for a variety across the land. Sofrito, a culinary term that originally referred to a specific combination of sauteed or braised aromatics, exists in Latin American cuisine. It refers to a sauce of tomatoes, roasted bell peppers, garlic, onions and herbs. Latin American beverages are just as distinct as their foods. Some of the beverages can even date back to the times of the Native Americans. Some popular beverages include mate, pisco, horchata, chicha, atole, cacao and aguas frescas. Desserts in Latin America are generally very sweet in taste. They include dulce de leche, alfajor, rice pudding, tres leches cake, Teja and flan.

HAMBURGER (AMERICA)

Hamburgers are America's favorite grilled food. The term 'Hamburger' originally derives from the German town of Hamburg, Germany's second largest city, from where many emigrants came to America. Residents of Hamburg, New York, named after Hamburg Germany, attribute the invention of hamburgers to the Menches brothers, vendors at the 1885 County Fair. Today, the hamburgers are usually a feature of fast food restaurants in U.S.A. and many other countries. Traditionally, hamburgers are made with ground meat, but Chicken burgers are also gaining popularity, especially in India and many Asian countries.

Ingredients (Chicken Burger)
Serves 4

For The Patties:

1lb/500g chicken meat ground or finely chopped
1 half onion finely chopped
1 dash lemon juice
4 pinches paprika powder
2 pinches dried oregano
a little pepper, fresh ground is better
a little salt
1 hand fresh bread crumbs
1 egg lightly whisked
1 quarter chicken stock block dissolved in a quarter cup water

For the Rolls:

4 rolls   lettuce
sliced tomato   mayonnaise
thinly sliced onion

Method

Mix all the patty ingredients thoroughly, leaving the salt for after the patties are cooked if you prefer.

Make sure the mixture is cool. Divide mixture into 4 equal balls and press into patties.

Cook on low heat under the grill, on the barbecue or in a pan until cooked through.

Split the rolls and toast the cut surfaces lightly (under grill, on barbecue or in pan) just before the patties are done. Spread mayonnaise on the bottom half, add a thin slice of onion, some lettuce and sliced tomato. Top it off with a little mayo, the patty and the other half of the roll.

Brush the hamburger and hot dog buns with melted butter and toast them briefly on the grill, if desired.

CHICKEN SHAWARMA (CANADA)

Canadian cuisine varies widely from region to region. Generally, the traditional cuisine of English Canada is closely related to British and American cuisine, while the traditional cuisine of French Canada has evolved from French cuisine. The basis of both groups is seasonal, fresh ingredients and preserves. The cuisine includes baked foods, wild game, and gathered foods. While most major cities in Canada (other than Montreal, due to local by-laws) offer a variety of street food, regional "specialties" are notable. Montreal offers a number of specialties including Shish taouk, the Montreal hot dog. Although falafel is widespread in Vancouver, 99 cent pizza slices are much more popular. Shawarma is quite prevalent in Ottawa, and Windsor.

Ingredients

* 1/4 cup lime juice
* 1/4 cup olive oil
* 1 tablespoon allspice toasted and ground
* 1 tablespoon coriander seed toasted and ground
* 1 garlic clove, minced
* 1 tablespoon fresh chopped summer savory
* 1 onion, grated
* 2 pounds chicken thighs, skin removed, bones removed and pounded to even thickness
* Coarse salt and freshly cracked black pepper

Yogurt Dressing

* 2 tablespoons lemon juice
* 1 cup yogurt
* 1/2 cup chopped fresh flat-leaf (Italian) parsley
* Coarse salt and freshly cracked black pepper

Assembly

* 6 thick pitas
* 1 large tomato, thinly sliced
* 6 leaves Boston lettuce

Directions

Chicken

1. Combine the lime juice, olive oil, spices, garlic, summer savory and grated onion in a medium bowl.
2. Add the chicken thighs and toss to coat.
3. Cover with plastic and marinate in the refrigerator for four hours.
4. Preheat the barbecue on medium.
5. Remove the chicken from the marinade, shaking off any excess.
6. Skewer the thighs on a long metal skewer, stacking them flat on top of each other.
7. Season the chicken thighs and put them on the grill.
8. Cover and cook the chicken, turning the skewer every few minutes for even cooking, 25 to 30 minutes or until charred on the outside and chicken is cooked through and juices run clear.

Yogurt Dressing

1. In a small bowl, combine the lemon juice, yogurt, parsley and some salt and pepper.
2. Refrigerate, covered in plastic until ready to use.

Assembly

Slice chicken off the skewer in thin shavings and serve it wrapped in pita bread along with the tomato slices, lettuce and Yogurt Dressing.

BURRITOS (MEXICO)

Burritos are one of the most popular examples of Mexican cuisine outside of Mexico. It consists of a flour tortilla wrapped or folded around a filling. The flour tortilla is usually lightly grilled or steamed, to soften it and make it more pliable. In Mexico, refried beans, Mexican rice, or meat are usually the only fillings and the tortilla is smaller in size. In the United States, however, fillings generally include a combination of ingredients such as Mexican rice, beans, lettuce, salsa, meat, avocado, cheese, and sour cream, and the size varies, with some burritos considerably larger than their Mexican counterparts. For most Mexican food lovers burritos evoke pacifying comfort food qualities that soothe the soul. Touted for their health benefits, black bean burritos are also a good source of dietary fiber.

Ingredients:

6 large (8-or 9-inch) tortillas
1 tablespoon oil
1 small onion, chopped
1 garlic clove, minced
1 (10-ounce) can chicken breast chunks, drained
1/2 (15 1/2-ounce) can black beans, drained and rinsed
1 cup cooked long-grain white rice
1 (14 1/2-ounce) can diced tomatoes 8 ounces shredded Jack or Cheddar cheese
Chopped cilantro or scallions for garnish, optional

Method

Wrap tortillas in foil and place in oven; heat to 400 degrees. Meanwhile, heat oil in 10-inch skillet over medium heat. Add onion and garlic and cook, stirring until softened. Stir in chicken, breaking up meat slightly. Stir in beans, rice and tomatoes.

Unwrap warmed tortillas. Spoon about ¾ cup of the filling in the center of the tortilla, leaving an inch at either end. Sprinkle ¼ cup shredded cheese on top, fold in 1-inch ends, then roll tortilla around filling. Place in a large shallow baking dish. Repeat with remaining tortillas.

Sprinkle remaining cheese on top of burritos. Cover with foil and heat in oven for about 10 minutes, until cheese is melted and filling is hot.

For a garnish, sprinkle with cilantro and/or scallion.

Note: For extra flavor, cook rice with chicken broth instead of water; use canned tomatoes and chilies for a spicier taste. For a recipe somewhat lower in fat, use reduced-fat cheese.

TAMALES (MEXICO)

A tamale is a traditional Mexican dish consisting of steam-cooked corn dough with a filling. Their essence is the corn meal dough, usually filled with sweet or savory filling, wrapped in plant leaves or corn husks, and cooked, usually by steaming, until firm. Considered by Mexicans one of their most beloved traditional foods, few countries have such an extensive variety of tamales as Mexico. Almost every region and state in the country has its own kind of tamale. The versatile nature of Tamales allows them to be prepared in more sophisticated ways among Mexican upscale chefs. Today, tamales are mainly consumed as comfort food in Mexico and is also eaten during festivities, such as the Day of the Dead, Posadas and Mexican Independence Day.

Ingredients

Dough

¼ cup water
4 cups freshly grated corn
½ cup ground yellow cornmeal
2 teaspoons sugar
1 teaspoon salt
1 tablespoon butter

Filling

1 clove garlic
½ teaspoon salt
½ teaspoon black pepper
1lb ground lamb or chicken
2 teaspoons olive oil

1 teaspoon wine vinegar
1 tablespoon vegetable oil
1 onion finely chopped
½ green bell pepper, seeded and chopped
2 hard boiled eggs, chopped
2 tablespoons seedless raisins
8 olives, sliced
1 tablespoon tomato puree
2 tablespoons oil

To cook

30 cornhusks or 30 5-inch foil squares
1 bay leaf 1 spring cilantro
1 teaspoon ground cumin

Method

For Dough:

Blend water and grated corn to form a paste. Place in a saucepan with cornmeal, sugar, salt and butter. Cook, stirring until mixture thickens and almost forms dough, about 20 minutes. Set aside for at least one hour.

For filling:

Mash garlic, salt and pepper together thoroughly to make a paste. Mix into ground lamb or chicken with olive oil and vinegar. Set aside.

Heat vegetable oil in a saucepan over medium heat. Add onion and bell pepper and cook, stirring occasionally, until onion is transparent, about 5 to 8 minutes. Add meat mixture and brown, about 10 minutes, stirring occasionally. Add eggs, raisins, olives, tomato puree and 1 teaspoon oil. Reduce heat to low and cook for 5 more minutes.

Grease each cornhusk or piece of foil with oil. Place a heaping spoonful of the corn dough in the middle and spread to within ½ inch of the edges using back of a spoon. Place a spoonful of the meat mixture in the middle of the dough, then fold the husk or foil so that the sides of the corn mixture seal in the meat. Fasten each parcel with piece of string.

Bring 20 cups water to boil with bay leaf, cilantro, cumin and salt. Add tamales and simmer 1 hour over medium heat. Lift out with a slotted spoon, then unwrap and serve hot.

LLAPINGACHOS (ECUADOR)

Ecuador is situated in South America and it is covered with wide fields, jungles, tropical forests and agricultural plains. Because of this, the Ecuadorian people are in touch with the nature and all its elements. There are many fruits and vegetables growing in the country, so the Ecuadorian people are familiar to them and know how to use them best. Ecuador's locals are very proud of their national plants and aliments that are unified in their cuisine; a cuisine which is exotic, highly flavored and spiritually meaningful. At only pennies per bite, bakeries offer a delicious range of breads, sweet pastries, and savory snacks, such as empanadas (hot, crispy meat or cheese-filled pastries) and llapingachos (potato and cheese pancakes). Tortillas de maiz (thin corn pancakes) and choclo (barbecued Andean corn) are sold by street vendors and make great snacks any time of day.

Ingredients

* Russet potatoes, peeled—2 pounds
* White cheese, shredded—1 cup
* Scallions, chopped finely—6
* Salt—to taste
* Achiote powder (see notes)—2 teaspoons
* Oil—1/4 cup

Method

1. Place the potatoes in a large saucepan, cover with salted water and bring to a boil, uncovered, over medium-high heat. Cook the potatoes until a knife pierces them easily. Drain the potatoes and set them aside to steam dry for 3 to 4 minutes.

2. Mash the potatoes until smooth or put them through a ricer. Season to taste with salt. When cool enough, form 1/3 cup portions of the mashed potatoes into balls and set on a baking sheet. Chill for at least 20 minutes; this will make the patties much easier to handle.

3. Remove potatoes from the refrigerator. Mix the cheese and scallions together and stuff each ball with about 1 tablespoon of the mixture. Flatten the balls with your hands to form patties.

4. Heat the oil in a skillet over medium heat. Sauté the patties, a few at a time, until browned on each side. Remove to a warm oven until all patties have been sautéed.

Variations

* The achiote powder gives the patties an orange color. If you don't have achiote, add a teaspoon or two of paprika. Or just leave it out altogether.

* Ecuadorans typically use a young white cheese called queso blanco for stuffing llapingachos, but you can use Monterey jack or mozzarella.

* Use finely minced white onion instead of scallions.

* Mix the cheese and scallions in with the potatoes instead of stuffing them.

CACHAPAS (VENZUELA)

Cachapas are rib-sticking pancakes made with fresh corn. They are sold as road-side snacks in Venezuela, wrapped around chopped ham or spread with butter, cream cheese or sour cream. Cachapas are a great, gluten-free option for people who who want a change from pancakes made with wheat flour.

Ingredients

* Corn kernels, fresh or frozen—4 cups (about 1 1/2 pounds)
* Cornstarch—1/2 cup
* Melted butter or olive oil—2 tablespoons
* Sugar—1 tablespoon
* Salt—2 teaspoons
* Water—as needed

Method

1. If using frozen corn, thaw it first. Add the corn, cornstarch, butter or oil, sugar and salt to a food processor or blender and process until fairly smooth but still a little chunky. Add water as needed to give the batter a consistency a little thicker than heavy cream.
2. Heat a heavy skillet over medium flame. Wipe the skillet with a little oil or butter and add about 1/2 cup of the batter to the skillet and spread it out a bit. Turn when the surface bubbles and the bottoms are golden brown, about 2 to 2 1/2 minutes, and brown on the other side.
3. Hold in a warm oven and repeat with the remaining batter. Serve hot, spread with butter or folded around your favorite filling.

EMPANADAS PAISAS (COLUMBIA)

Colombian is blessed with a rich natural space, a variety of the fauna and flora and a high agricultural potential. The most significant agricultural possessions are the coffee plantations (Colombia is the second exporter in the world, but Colombian coffee is recognized as the best one), banana trees, cocoa, beans and sugar cane. Combining the Spanish cuisine with that of the Africans and the Native Americans, the Colombian cuisine is known for its exoticness and spicy taste. There are many fried dishes, as frying seems to be the most frequent preparation method of the Colombian cooking: fried puff squares (hojuelas), fried plantains, fried cheese puffs (bunuelos) and various kinds of fried meat. Empanadas Paisas (meat-filled turnovers with cumin seed and brown sugar) is a popular snack throughout Columbia.

Ingredients:

1 lb of lean meat two large red potatoes
* two eggs
* small onion
* 2 cloves cut up garlic
* bay leaf
* salt

Directions:

Place meat, potatoes and eggs in enough water to cover them. Add the small cut up onion, garlic, bay leafand salt. Bring to boil, then lower to simmer. In about 1/2 hour when the potatoes are tender and the eggs are hard boiled, remove them. Simmer the meat for at least another hour.

Remove meat and cool completely.

Preparation of the meat filling:

Grind the cooked meat in a food grinder, or in a food processor. Chop the potatoes and the eggs finely. Add the eggs and potatoes to the ground meat. Now you must prepare a spicy "hogao" sauce to add to the meat mixture.

Hogao

Ingredients:

* 2 large tomatoes, finely chopped
* 4 green onions, finely chopped
* 3 cloves garlic, minced
* 1 tblsp of cilantro, minced
* salt to taste
* 3 tblsp of olive oil

Directions:

Heat oil in a saucepan and add all of the ingredients. Cook over medium heat until everything is mushy. Add this "hogao" sauce to the meat mixture. You will need to add some broth left over from cooking the meat, in order to get the meat filling moist. You don't want the filling to be dry.

Preparation of the corn dough:

Salt to taste 3 cups of boiling water, plus a tablespoon of brown sugar. Pour the boiling hot water in a heat proof container, stirring constantly, slowly pour in the 2 cups of yellow corn meal, this will get pretty thick and hard to stir towards the end. Try to knead it as much as you can with the spoon, but eventually, as the dough cools, you can knead it with your hands. When the dough looks pretty smooth, about 5 minutes of kneading, cover it with a plastic or moist towel to keep it from drying out.

In a heavy deep frying pan, pour about 3 inches of oil. Start heating the oil over medium/high heat.

Shape dough into the size of small golf balls. You can do this golf ball shaping ahead of time as long as you keep them covered. Flatten a ball with a flat object such a a plate sprayed with Pam, also spray the surface underneath. Place a heaping tablespoon of meat filling on one hemisphere of the flattened dough. Fold the other half over and pinch together so that there is NO opening showing any filling. Place carefully in the hot oil and fry until golden brown. Drain on papers towels and serve immediately with lime quarters or sauce of your choice.

EMPANADAS (ARGENTINA)

The cuisine of Argentina is distinctive in South America because of its strong resemblance to Spanish, Italian, French and other European cuisines. Another determining factor in Argentine cuisine is that the country is one of the world's major food producers. It is a major producer of meat, wheat, corn, milk, beans, and since the 1970s, soybeans. Argentines are famous for their high protein diet. Grilled meat from the asado (barbecue) is a staple. Empanadas—small pastries of meat, cheese, sweet corn and a hundred other varieties—are a common sight for parties, starters and picnics across Argentina.

Ingredients:

* 1 pound meat steak
* 1/2 cup vegetable oil
* 1 cup chopped white onion
* 2 cloves garlic, finely chopped
* 1 teaspoon cumin
* 2 teaspoons paprika
* 1/4-1/2 teaspoon chili powder
* 1 teaspoon salt
* 3 green onions, white and green parts sliced crosswise into thin rings
* salt and pepper to taste
* 2 1/2 teaspoons salt
* 1/2-3/4 cup water
* 4 1/2 cups flour
* 3/4 cup lard or vegetable shortening

Preparation:

For the Filling:

1. Finely chop the meat into 1 cm. square pieces.
2. Cook the garlic and the white onions in oil until tender.
3. Add the paprika, cumin, salt, and chili pepper, and stir well.
4. Add the meat and cook until just browned. Add 1/2 to 1 cup water and simmer for 5-10 minutes more, allowing water to boil off. The filling should be juicy but not watery, and the meat should be tender.
5. Stir in the green onions and sauté 1 minute more. Season with salt and pepper to taste.
6. Chill meat mixture for 2 to 24 hours.

Make the dough:

1. Sift the salt with the flour into a bowl.
2. Using a pastry cutter or your fingers, cut the lard or shortening into the flour until well blended. Slowly stir in the water a little at a time, reserving some.
3. Turn the dough out onto a flat surface and knead, adding more water if necessary until the dough comes together into smooth clump. If you add too much water and the dough is too sticky, you can knead in some more flour.
4. Knead the dough for 5 to 10 minutes, until it is smooth and stretchy. The dough should not be sticky at all. Cover dough with a dish towel and let dough relax at room temperature for 30 minutes. You can wrap the dough in plastic warp and keep in the refrigerator overnight.

Shape the empanandas:

1. Preheat the oven to 450 degrees.
2. Roll out half the dough very thin, to 1/4" thick. Cut the dough into 4-5 inch rounds, using a large cookie cutter, bowl, or coffee can. Knead the scraps into a ball and let the dough rest, covered,

while you roll out the other half of dough. You should end up with 20 to 24 rounds, depending on the size.

3. Place 1-2 tablespoons of filling in the middle of a dough round. Brush edges of circle with water. Fold the round in half over the filling, and press down hard along the edges to seal.

4. Starting at one end of the pressed-down edge, fold the edge towards the middle and press down. Move your fingers over 1/2 inch and fold the edge into the middle again. Continue around the sealed edge of the empanada, folding the edge over itself, to make a twisted rope effect.

5. Bake the empanadas for 10 minutes, then turn the temperature down to 400 degrees and bake for 10-15 minutes more. The empanadas should be golden brown.

6. Store baked empanadas in the refrigerator or freezer and reheat in the microwave. Unbaked empanadas can also be frozen.

ALCAPURRIAS (PUERTO RICO)

Say the word "alcapurrias," and most Puerto Ricans think "beach food." These scrumptious fritters are usually made with a batter of taro (yautía) and green bananas (guineos verdes), and are stuffed with either a meat (pino) filling or with crab, shrimp or lobster. Sold by vendors on the beach, they make a great snack for hungry stomachs after a long day in the sun.

Ingredients

* Yautía (taro root)—1 pound
* Green bananas—4
* Sazón seasoning (optional)—2 teaspoons
* Salt—1 teaspoon
* Pino filling—2 cups
* Oil for deep frying

Method

1. Peel the yautía and grate it on a fine grater into a large bowl. Next peel the green bananas and grate them into the same bowl. Add the sazón and salt and mix together well. Place the masa, or batter, in a food processor and pulse until the batter is fairly smooth.
2. Cut a banana leaf or a piece of wax or parchment paper into a round slightly larger than your hand. Put about 1/2 cup of the batter onto the round and spread it out a bit. Place 2 to 3 tablespoons of the pino filling in the middle of the batter. Using the round, fold the batter up and around the filling, completely enclosing it. Form the batter into a smooth, oval round and set it aside. Continue with the remaining batter and filling until it is used up.

3. Heat about 2 inches of oil in a large pan or deep fryer to about 370°F. Drop a few of the alcapurrias at a time into the oil and fry until well browned on one side. Flip and brown well on the second side. Remove to a paper towel-lined plate and repeat with the remaining alcapurrias.

4. Serve hot with a hefty dash of hot pepper sauce.

5. To shape the patties, take a large soup spoon and fill the bowl of the spoon with some of the batter, pressing it firmly into the spoon. Sprinkle the top with sesame seeds and then push it off the spoon into the hot oil.

6. Fry for 2 to 3 minutes or until it has turned brown. Turn the patties over and cook again 2 to 3 minutes or until brown. Remove from the oil to a paper towel to drain. Don't let the oil get too hot or the crust will get too crisp or if the oil cools down too much, the patties will soak up too much oil.

EMPANADAS DE PINO (CHILE)

Empanadas are the most favorite of Chile snacks. There is a food vendor on just about every street corner in South America, selling Chilean Empanadas. In Chile, the most traditional empanada filling is called "pino". Pino is a seasoned mixture of ground meat, onions, raisins, black olives, and hard boiled eggs. The empananda dough1 is quick and easy to make, and can be made ahead and stored in the refrigerator. The pino tastes best if made the day before and allowed to rest overnight before filling the empanandas.

Ingredients:

* Empanada dough (see recipe below)
* 3 large onions, chopped
* 1 pound ground meat
* 2 teaspoons cumin
* 1 teaspoon chile powder
* 1 tablespoon paprika
* 2 tablespoons flour
* 1/2 cup raisins
* 1/2 cup chopped olives
* 2 hard boiled eggs, sliced
* 1 egg yolk
* 2 tablespoons milk

Preparation:

1. Prepare empanada dough2 and chill.
2. Cook the onions and garlic in the vegetable oil and butter until softened. Add the ground meat, cumin, chile powder, paprika and salt and pepper to taste.

3. Cook the meat, stirring and crumbling the meat, until browned. Add the flour and continue to cook for 5 or 10 minutes more.
4. Remove the meat mixture and let cool. The meat mixture will keep up to 2 days in the refrigerator.
5. Shape the empanadas: Separate the dough into golf ball size pieces, and roll into smooth balls. Let rest for 5 minutes. On a floured surface, roll each ball of dough into a 6 inch diameter circle, about 1/4 inch thick. Add 1 tablespoon of the meat filling, a few raisins and some chopped olives, and a slice of hard boiled egg to the middle of the circle.
6. Brush the edges with water and fold the pastry in half over the filling, to make a semi-circle.
7. Seal the edges by pressing down with your fingers. Brush the sealed edge lightly with water, then turn the edge toward the middle and press with your fingers to seal.
8. Mix the egg yolk with 2 tablespoons milk, and brush the empanadas with the mixture.
9. Bake at 350 for 25-30 minutes, or until golden brown.

Empanada Dough

This recipe produces a sweet dough that contrasts perfectly with savory fillings. Empanada dough is less flaky than pie crust (although you can substitute frozen pie crust dough in a pinch)—it has a tender texture that soaks up the filling.

This dough can be used for baked or fried empananadas. If you are going to fry the empanadas, omit the egg yolk and roll the dough out slightly thinner (less than 1/4" thickness).

Ingredients:

* 4 cups flour
* 1-2 teaspoons salt
* 2-3 tablespoons sugar
* 2 tablespoons butter, softened

* 12 tablespoons lard or vegetable shortening, at room temperature
* 3/4 cup cup water
* 2 egg yolks

Preparation:

1. Sift the flour into a bowl. Stir in the salt and the sugar.
2. Work the butter and shortening or lard into the flour mixture with your fingers until well blended.
3. Whisk the egg yolks into the water. Stir in the 1/2 cup of water/ egg mixture, a little at a time until the dough comes together smoothly. Keep kneading the dough, adding more water/egg a little bit at a time as necessary (you made need more than 1 cup), until the dough is very smooth, about 5-10 minutes. You can knead the dough with a standing mixer and a dough hook attachment.
4. Cover the dough with saran wrap and let rest on the counter for about an hour. (Dough can also be kept overnight in the refrigerator, then brought to room temperature before using.) Dough should be soft and smooth, and not elastic—if you poke a hole in it with your finger, the indentation should remain.
5. Turn dough out onto a floured surface, and roll into desired thickness.
6. Makes enough dough for 8 large empanadas.

CROQUETAS DE BATATA (CUBA)

On the Spanish speaking islands appetizers are called aperitivos and snacks are called bocados. In the Caribbean they have their own sweet potato called a batata or boniato. This sweet potato fritter (croquetas de batata) is an easy recipe for beginners and a hit with anyone who likes sweet potatoes. Make these small fried sweet potato rolls for an appetizer, party snack, or side dish.

Ingredients:

* 3 cups sweet potatoes (cooked and mashed)
* 2 tablespoons butter
* 1 teaspoon salt
* 2 eggs
* 1/4 teaspoon cinnamon
* 1/4 cup sugar
* 3 eggs (beaten for egg wash)
* 1 1/2 cups bread crumbs
* oil for frying

Preparation:

1. Heat oil on a deep frying pan or deep fryer to about 360 ferenheit.
2. In a large bowl thoroughly mix together the sweet potatoes, butter, salt, 2 eggs, cinnamon and sugar.
3. Shape the mixture into croquettes (small rolls).
4. Roll the croquettes in the bread crumbs, then the egg wash, and then in bread crumbs again.
5. Fry the croquettes in oil until golden (a couple minutes per side). Be careful not to burn.
6. Remove from the oil and drain on paper towels.
7. Serve warm.

BOLO SALGADO (BRAZIL)

Brazil is a large country that is made up of many different cultures. Each region has a different food specialty. During Carnival, colorful parades are held on the streets, and children and adults dress in costumes, dancing and celebrating in the streets all day and all night. People eat and drink continuously during Carnival, enjoying Brazilian snacks that are mostly light and easy to prepare, such as Bolo Solgado (Brazilian Casserole).

Ingredients:

* 2 cups flour
* 1 tbsp. baking powder
* 1 1/2 tsp. salt
* 2 cups milk
* 1 egg
* 1/4 cup grated cheese

Method:

Mix well. In another bowl, mix together 1 cup of the following vegetables, chopped (tomato, onion, green pepper, green onion, garlic clove). Mix with 1 tablespoon vinegar and 1/2 teaspoon salt. Pour into greased 9 x 13 inch pan. Bake in 350 degree oven about 25 to 30 minutes until browned and somewhat firm on top (will be softer inside when you serve it).

THE CONTINENT OF EUROPE

European cuisine, or alternatively Western cuisine, is a generalized term collectively referring to the cuisines of Europe and other Western countries. The cuisines of Western countries are diverse by themselves, although there are common characteristics that distinguishes Western cooking from cuisines of Asian countries and others. Compared with traditional cooking of Asian countries, for example, meat is more prominent and substantial in serving-size. Steak in particular is a common dish across the West. Similarly to some Asian cuisines, Western cuisines also put substantial emphasis on sauces as condiments, seasonings, or accompaniments (in part due to the difficulty of seasonings penetrating the often larger pieces of meat used in Western cooking). Many dairy products are utilized in the cooking process. Wheat-flour bread has long been the most common sources of starch in this cuisine, along with pasta, dumplings and pastries, although the potato has become a major starch plant in the diet of Europeans and their diaspora since the European colonisation of the Americas. Maize is much less common in most European diets than it is in the Americas; however corn meal, or polenta, is a major part of the cuisine of Italy and the Balkans.

The northern European diet generally consists of a large serving of meat, poultry, or fish, accompanied by small side dishes of vegetables and starch. The traditional diet is high in protein, primarily from meat and dairy products. The diet tends to be low in whole grains, fruits, and vegetables. Immigrants from this region of the world brought this eating pattern to North America and it still influences the "meat and potatoes" American meal. The influence of each country's food habits on each other is also extensive.

English cuisine was primarily shaped during the Victorian era. The diet relies heavily on meats, dairy products, wheat, and root vegetables. The English are famous for their flower gardens, but they are also known for their kitchen gardens, which yield an abundance of herbs and vegetables.

Breakfast is very hearty and generally consists of bacon, eggs, grilled tomato, and fried bread. Kippers (smoked herring) are also popular at breakfast. Many Britons still partake in afternoon tea, which consists of tiny sandwiches (no crust) filled with cucumber or watercress, scones or crumpets with jam or clotted cream, cakes or tarts, and a pot of hot tea. Tea shops abound in England, Wales, and Scotland, and Britons drink about four cups of tea a day. Coffee is also very popular with the younger generation.

Milk, cheese, meat, cereals, and some vegetables formed the main part of the Irish diet before the potato was introduced to Ireland in the seventeenth century. The Irish were the first Europeans to use the potato as a staple food. The potato, more than anything else, contributed to the population growth on the island, which had less than 1 million inhabitants in the 1590s but had 8.2 million in 1840. However, the dependency on the potato eventually led to two major famines and a series of smaller famines. The potato is still the staple food in Ireland, though other root vegetables, such as carrots, turnips, and onions, are eaten when in season. A traditional Irish dish is colcannon, made of mashed potatoes, onions, and cabbage.

One of modern France's greatest treasures is its rich cuisine. The French have an ongoing love affair with food. Families still gather together for the Sunday midday feast, which is eaten leisurely through a number of appetizers and main courses. Most French meals are accompanied by wine. French cuisine is divided into classic French cuisine (haute cuisine) and provincial or regional cuisine. Classic French cuisine is elegant and formal and is mostly prepared in restaurants and catered at parties. More simple meals are usually prepared at home. Buttery, creamy sauces characterize classic French cuisine in the west, northwest, and north-central regions. The area surrounding Paris in the north-central region is the home of classic French cuisine. German cuisine has influenced French cuisine in the east and northeast parts of the country. Beer, sausage, sauerkraut, and goose are very popular, for example. Olive oil, tomatoes, garlic, herbs, and fresh vegetables are all widely used. Famous dishes from this region are black truffeles, ratatouille, salade Niçoise, and bouillabaisse.

East European food consists largely of wonderful stews and soups, pirogs and other baked delices and plates of cold cuts and salads. When we talk about Russian Cuisine, it is never complete without Shashlyk which is a famous kind of barbecue Kebab and it is the hot favorite dish not only in Russia but in Mongolia and throughout former states of the then Soviet Union.

FISH 'N' CHIPS (ENGLAND)

Fish 'n' Chips come from England, and you can't imagine an English town without a Fish and Chip shop. Before the onslaught of Indian Chicken Tikka Masala, Fish 'n' Chips remained England's number one national snack. It is not as hard as you might think to create your own perfect Fish 'n' Chips at home. It just takes a little preparation time, that's all. The actual cooking is done in just a few minutes and the preparation time can also be measured in minutes. You can use any kind of fish with this recipe, but for genuine English Fish 'n' Chips, it is best to use a white fish such as Cod or Haddock. The fish, although it is deep fried, actually cooks inside the batter, and is really steamed because it never touches the oil, just the batter does. You can't really call it a low fat recipe, but if the oil is hot, the fish is very crispy, holds very little fat and tastes steamed. Most people eat fish 'n' chips with tomato ketchup, but the English sprinkle dark vinegar (malt vinegar) over the fish 'n' chips.

Ingredients

1 1/2 pounds potatoes, washed and peeled
2 pounds fillets of cod or haddock
Seasoned flour for dredging
Oil (for deep-frying)
1 egg (at room temperature)
1 cup water
1 cup self-rising flour
1/2 teaspoon salt
Freshly-ground pepper

Method

Start preparing exactly 40 minutes before serving time. Slice potatoes into long sticks about 1/4-inch thick. Put sticks into a bowl and cover with ice cold water to soak. This will remove some of the starch and will result in a crispier and less fattening French fry.

Prepare the batter by breaking the egg into a large mixing bowl and lightly whisk with the water. Still whisking, add the flour, a little at a time. Make sure all lumps of flour are beaten out so that you finish up with a smooth consistency. Add salt and ground pepper and set aside.

Thoroughly wash the fish fillets under cold running water. Check to ensure that all bones have been removed. Divide the fish into 8 equal pieces? 2 per serving. Carefully dry with paper towels and dredge each piece in seasoned flour, shaking off the excess. Heat oil to 375 degrees F to 400 degrees F. At the same time heat up 1 inch of oil in a heavy-bottom frying pan to the same temperature.

While the fat is slowly getting up to temperature, drain the potatoes, getting as much moisture from them as possible with paper towels. Dip each piece of fish into the batter mixture. Allow excess batter to drip back into the bowl and gently immerse the fillet in the hot oil. Do not cook more than 2 or 3 pieces of fish at a time. The inside of the fish will be cooked when the outside batter is a mid to light brown. Turn the oven to low so that you can keep the cooked pieces of fish warm while the others are cooking.

Take 2 handsful of potatoes and carefully release them into the deep-fryer. When golden brown, remove with a slotted spoon so that you can shake off the excess oil, and turn onto paper towels.

Season lightly with salt and serve wrapped in a newspaper cone with malt vinegar and/or ketchup.

CURRYWURST (GERMANY)

Germany's most popular snack, the 'currywurst'—literally, "curried fried sausage"—now has a museum dedicated to itself in Berlin. 60 years since it was invented, this urban snack has a cult following—800 million are eaten in Germany every year. Herta Heuwer, who invented the quick snack, certainly never expected her culinary creation—bite-sized pieces of sausage covered in curry-flavoured ketchup—to prove a hit with so many people. When she made Germany's new favourite meal for the first time on 4th September 1949, it was just a way of passing time, though decades later it has become a classic, in Germany and around the world.

Ingredients:

3 (15 ounce) cans tomato sauce
1 pound sausages
2 tablespoons chili sauce
1/2 teaspoon onion salt
1 tablespoon white sugar
1 teaspoon ground black pepper
1 pinch paprika
Curry powder to taste

Directions:

1. Preheat oven to Broil/Grill.
2. Pour tomato sauce into a large saucepan, then stir in the chili sauce, onion salt, sugar and pepper. Let simmer over medium heat, occasionally stirring; bring to a gentle boil and reduce heat to low. Simmer another 5 minute.
3. Meanwhile, broil/grill sausages for 3 to 4 minutes each side, or until cooked through. Slice into pieces 1/4 inch to 1/2 inch thick. Pour tomato sauce mixture over sausage, then sprinkle all with paprika and curry powder and serve.

BUTTER ROLLS (DENMARK)

If you like butter, you'll love these simple but delicious Danish butter rolls—Smørdejgssnitter. They're baked in a sweet milk sauce. Just the thing for a cold morning. Very easy to make, great flavor and fabulous melt in your mouth texture. A terrific recipe for slightly sweet, fluffy crescent rolls. They're a bit more dense than a croissant but much lighter than an average dinner roll. These rolls take a while to make (the dough rises in the refrigerator overnight), but can be done well ahead of time . . . and they're certainly worth the effort.

Ingredients

* ¼ cup boiling water
* ½ cup butter
* ¼ cup cream
* ½ teaspoon salt
* 3 eggs—beaten
* 1 teaspoon vanilla
* 2 packages dry yeast
* 1 tablespoon Sugar
* 3 cups flour
* 1 cup nuts—ground
* ½ cup Sugar

Directions

Pour the water over the butter. Cool. Add cream, salt, eggs, vanilla and the yeast mixed with the tablespoon Sugar. Let it stay 10 minutes. Add the flour. The dough will be stiff but not sticky.

Let it rise in a warm place until doubled in bulk. Punch down. Cut off pieces of dough with a spoon and roll in the ground nuts mixed with the Sugar. Twist each piece into a figure 8. Place on greased baking sheets and let it rest 10 minutes.

Bake in a preheated 450º oven 10 to 15 minutes.

CHEESE SOUFFLE (FRANCE)

This puffy dish of cheese and eggs is one of the most popular snacks originating in France and now favorite internationally. These individual souffles are elegant for brunch. A classic, pillowy cheese soufflé turns supper into an act of kindness worth bestowing on yourself. It is the perfect antidote for a mental low down. A couple of bites into this mind altering dish and the low down is a thing of the past. You're rejuvenated, ready to take on the world. It's easy to make, goes great with a baby romaine, avocado and sliced Ruby Red Grapefruit salad with a Dijon mustard vinaigrette.

Ingredients

You need soufflé moulds, well buttered and floured

* Butter, room temperature, for greasing the souffle
* 2 tablespoons grated Parmesan
* 1 1/2 ounces (3 tablespoons) butter
* 3 tablespoons flour
* 1 teaspoon dry mustard
* 1/2 teaspoon garlic powder
* 1/8 teaspoon kosher salt
* 1 1/3 cups milk, hot
* 4 large egg yolks (2 1/2 ounces by weight)
* 6 ounces sharp Cheddar
* 5 egg whites plus 1 tablespoon water
* 1/2 teaspoon cream of tartar

Directions

Use room temperature butter to grease souffle mold. Add the grated Parmesan and roll around the mold to cover the sides. Cover with plastic wrap and place into the freezer for 5 minutes.

Preheat oven to 375 degrees F.

In a small saucepan, heat the butter. Allow all of the water to cook out.

In a separate bowl combine the flour, dry mustard, garlic powder, and kosher salt. Whisk this mixture into the melted butter. Cook for 2 minutes.

Whisk in the hot milk and turn the heat to high. Once the mixture reaches a boil, remove from the heat.

In a separate bowl, beat the egg yolks to a creamy consistency. Temper the yolks into the milk mixture, constantly whisking. Remove from the heat and add the cheese. Whisk until incorporated.

In a separate bowl, using a hand mixer, whip the egg whites and cream of tartar until glossy and firm. Add 1/4 of the mixture to the base. Continue to add the whites by thirds, folding very gently.

Pour the mixture into the souffle moulds. Fill the moulds to 1/2-inch from the top. Place on an aluminum pie pan. Bake in the oven for 35 minutes, then serve immediately.

PIZZA (ITALY)

Pizza is a world-popular dish of Italian origin, made with an oven-baked, flat, generally round bread that is often covered with tomatoes or a tomato-based sauce and cheese. Other toppings are added according to region, culture, or personal preference. In the 20th century pizza has become an international food with widely varying toppings. These pizzas consist of the same basic design but include an exceptionally diverse choice of ingredients. Pizza is an emerging fast food in Indian urban areas. With the arrival of branded pizza, it has reached to many cities. Pizza outlets serve pizzas with several Indian based toppings like Tandoori Chicken and Paneer. Indian pizzas are generally made more spicy as compared to their western counterparts, to suit Indian taste. Along with Indian variations, more conventional pizzas are also eaten.

Ingredients

Pizza Dough:

Makes enough dough for two 10-12 inch pizzas

* 1 1/2 cups warm water
* 2 1/4 teaspoons of active dry yeast
* 3 1/2 cups bread flour
* 2 tbsp olive oil
* 2 teaspoons salt
* 1 teaspoon sugar

Pizza Ingredients

* Olive oil
* Cornmeal (to slide the pizza onto the pizza stone)
* Tomato sauce

* Mozzarella or Parmesan cheese, shredded
* Feta cheese
* Mushrooms, thinly sliced
* Bell peppers, stems and seeds removed, thinly sliced
* Chopped fresh basil
* Onions, thinly sliced

Special equipment

* A pizza stone, highly recommended if you want your pizza dough to be crusty
* A pizza peel or a flat baking sheet
* A pizza wheel for cutting the pizza

Method

Making the Pizza Dough

1. In the large bowl, add the warm water. Sprinkle on the yeast and let sit for 5 minutes until the yeast is dissolved. Stir to dissolve completely if needed at the end of 5 minutes.
2. Mix in the olive oil, flour, salt and sugar on low speed for about a minute. Knead until the dough is smooth and elastic.
3. Place ball of dough in a bowl that has been coated lightly with olive oil. Turn the dough around in the bowl so that it gets coated with the oil. Cover with plastic wrap. Let sit in a warm place until it doubles in size, about 1 to 1 1/2 hours.

Preparing the Pizzas

1. Place a pizza stone on a rack in the lower third of your oven. Preheat the oven to 450°F for at least 30 minutes, preferably an hour.
2. Remove the plastic cover from the dough and punch the dough down so it deflates a bit. Divide the dough in half. Form two round balls of dough. Place each in its own bowl, cover with plastic and let sit for 10 minutes.

3. Prepare your desired toppings. Note that you are not going to want to load up each pizza with a lot of toppings as the crust will end up not crisp that way. About a third a cup each of tomato sauce and cheese would be sufficient for one pizza. One to two mushrooms thinly sliced will cover a pizza.

4. Working one ball of dough at a time, take one ball of dough and flatten it with your hands on a slightly floured work surface. Starting at the center and working outwards, use your fingertips to press the dough to 1/2-inch thick. Turn and stretch the dough until it will not stretch further. Let the dough relax 5 minutes and then continue to stretch it until it reaches the desired diameter—10 to 12 inches. Use your palm to flatten the edge of the dough where it is thicker.

5. Brush the top of the dough with olive oil (to prevent it from getting soggy from the toppings). Use your finger tips to press down and make dents along the surface of the dough to prevent bubbling. Let rest another 5 minutes.

Repeat with the second ball of dough.

6. Lightly sprinkle your pizza peel (or flat baking sheet) with corn meal. Transfer one prepared flattened dough to the pizza peel. If the dough has lost its shape in the transfer, lightly shape it to the desired dimensions.

7. Spoon on the tomato sauce, sprinkle with cheese, and place your desired toppings on the pizza.

8. Sprinkle some cornmeal on the baking stone in the oven. Slide the pizza on to the baking stone. Bake pizza one at a time until the crust is browned and the cheese is golden, about 10-15 minutes.

Remove from the oven and serve warm.

GNOCCHI DI PATATE (ITALY)

A classic Italian dumpling, Gnocchi Di Patate is featured in a lot of Northern Italian cuisine for a side dish or main dish, and is mostly known as gnocchi. It takes a little time to prepare them but they are easy to make and more than worth the effort. It's made by mixing mashed potatoes with flour and egg to form a thick, starchy pasta dough. This dough is rolled into ropes and then cut into individual nuggets before being boiled. Potato gnocchi should ideally have a light, springy texture, and they're great served in a simple sauce. In Verona every year they have a Gnocchi festival called "Venordi Gnocolar" during the carnival season, where it is a must to eat Gnocchi.

Ingredients

2 lb. floury potatoes
1 tablespoon butter
2 cups all purpose flour
2 eggs, well beaten
1 teaspoon salt
1/3 teaspoon freshly ground black pepper

Method

Preheat the oven to 350 F

Peel and dice the potatoes, then boil in lightly salted water for 20 minutes, or until tender. Mash until very smooth and blend in the butter.

Gradually work in the flour, beaten eggs and seasoning. Mix thoroughly but lightly.

Using floured hands, roll on a pastry board into finger-sized rolls. Cut into 1-in pieces.

Almost fill a large saucepan with water, heat to boiling, then reduce to a fast simmer. Drop in the gnocchi one by one and cook for 3 to 4 minutes.

Remove with slotted spoon as they rise to the surface and place in a heated ovenproof dish. Dot the gnocchi with butter and place in the warm oven only until the butter melts.

Serve plain or topped with a sauce of your choice.

POTATO CROQUETAS (SPAIN)

Potato Croquetas are the most popular part of tapas in Spain. Popular throughout Spain, tapas are appetizers and Spain's tastiest treats. They can also form an entire meal and range from simple items such as olives and cheese to more elaborate preparations like garlic shrimp and little meatballs. If so inclined, you can stuff some of the croquetas with cooked red pepper and onion. Serve these tasty potato croquetas with any combination of olives, nuts, cheese and fruits you desire.

Ingredients

* 1 lb large potato (about 2)
* 3 large eggs
* 1 tablespoon chopped fresh flat-leaf parsley
* 1 tablespoon finely chopped fresh chives
* 1/4 teaspoon chopped fresh tarragon
* 2 tablespoons unsalted butter, softened
* 1/2 teaspoon salt
* 1/8 teaspoon black pepper
* 3/4 cup flour
* 3/4 cup fine dry breadcrumb
* about 4 cups regular olive oil (for frying)

Directions

Peel potatoes and cut into 1-inch pieces. Cover with salted cold water by 1 inch in a 2-quart saucepan, then boil until tender, about 8 minutes.

Drain in a colander. Mash or force potatoes through a ricer into a medium bowl and cool.

Lightly beat 1 egg in a small bowl with a fork.

Add to cooled potatoes along with herbs, butter, salt, and pepper and stir until just combined.

Spoon tablespoons of potato mixture onto a tray, then lightly roll each into a ball between palms of your hands and return to tray.

Lightly beat remaining 2 eggs in a small bowl and set aside.

Spread flour in a shallow bowl, then spread bread crumbs in another shallow bowl.

Working in batches, roll balls in flour to coat, gently shaking off excess.

Dip balls in egg, turning to coat and letting excess drip off, then roll in bread crumbs and return to tray. Chill, covered, for 30 minutes.

Preheat oven to 200°F.

Heat 1 1/2 inches oil in a pot.

Working in batches, fry croquetas, turning if necessary, until browned, about 1 1/2 minutes per batch.

Transfer with a slotted spoon to paper towels to drain, then transfer to a baking pan and keep warm in the oven while frying remaining croquetas.

Croquetas can be fried up to 3 hours ahead and kept at room temperature. Reheat in a preheated 400°F oven for 8 minutes.

KOTLETY POJARSKIE (RUSSIA)

A specialty of Moscow, Kotlety Pojarskie (cutlets of ground chicken) is a dish that should seduce your guest, the most difficult. Cooking is a game but also a culture that is transmitted progressively. A landlord served it unexpectedly to the Tsar Nicolas I ready to move to St. Petersburg, and the dish remains a delighted glory in Russia since then.

Ingredients

3 thick slices bread, crusts removed
4 tablespoon milk
1 lb. ground chicken
1/3 cup butter, softened
½ teaspoon salt
1/3 spoon freshly ground black pepper
¼ teaspoon ground nutmeg 4 tablespoons flour
1 egg, beaten
1 ½ cup dry bread crumbs
Oil for cooking

Method:

Soak the bread slices in the milk, then squeeze as dry as possible. Blend together the chicken, butter and bread.

Add the salt, pepper and nutmeg and mix well. With lightly floured hands divide the mixture into 6 portions and form into cutlet shapes.

Dust lightly with flour, dip into the egg and then coat well with the bread crumbs.

Place on a plate or tray, cover and chill for 30 minutes.

Heat sufficient oil to generously cover the base of a large skillet and cook the cutlets for about 5 minutes each side, or until golden brown.

Serve piping hot.

ARNI SOUVLAKI (GREECE)

Arni Souvlaki (skewered lamb) is one of the most popular Greek snacks worldwide. Greek cooking offers an incredibly rich and diverse array of foods and beverages that are the culmination of literally thousands of years of living, cooking, and eating. While each Greek meal is fresh and inviting, it is also a trip back through Greece's history. Arni Souvlaki is simple and elegant, with flavors subtle to robust, textures smooth to crunchy, fresh and timeless, nutritious and healthy. Preparing and enjoying Greek food, anywhere in the world, is an adventurous journey into the cradle of civilization.

Ingredients

1 large leg of lamb
½ cup of olive oil
¼ cup lemon juice
4 garlic cloves
3 bay leaves, broken into pieces
Salt and pepper to taste
2 lemons cut into eighths
2 tablespoons parsley

Method

Cut all the meat from the bone and remove any fat. Cut the meat into 1-1/2 in cubes.

Combine all the remaining ingredients except the lemon and parsley in a large bowl.

Add the meat and stir well so that it is coated with the marinade.

Allow marinating in the refrigerator for about 24 hours, stirring occasionally.

Thread the meat onto skewers.

Cook under a hot broiler (griller) or on a barbecue, turning frequently until cooked, about 15 minutes.

Serve with the lemon wedges and a sprinkle of chopped parsley.

PELMENI (SERBIA)

In the Serbian cuisine, with the meat as the basic element, there are a lot of meals that can be considered as snacks. Bacon (slanina) is considered snack in the Serbian cuisine. It consists of certain cuts of meat taken from the sides or back of a pig, cured and sometimes smoked. Sandwiches are considered as great snacks, and are usually prepared with cheese and different types of hams and sausages, such as: Njeguški pršut, or Kulen. Pelmeni (Serbian Ravoli) is a popular snack that can also serve as a main meal.

Ingredients for the dough

200 gm all-purpose flour
1/2 teaspoon salt
2 eggs (lightly beaten)
80 ml water

Combine flour and salt and mound on a clean surface.

Make a well in the centre and add eggs and water.

Incorporate flour mixture with egg mixture by working around the walls of the well until the dough is mixed.

Knead on a floured surface until soft and pliable.

Form into 100 balls, cover with a moist towel and let rest at room temperature for one hour.

Ingredients for the filling

450 gm ground meat
1 onion (minced)
1 teaspoon dried dill
Salt and pepper
White of one small egg (beaten)
Water, chicken or meat broth
120 gm butter

Directions:

Mix ground meat, onion, dill, salt and pepper to taste and enough water to make a soft mixture.

When the dough is ready flatten the dough balls into circles with a diameter of 7.5 cm. Place one tablespoon filling on each dough round. Brush the edges with water and fold the dough to form half moons. Pinch opposite ends to one another to seal. Repeat this with the rest of the dough balls. Brush the pelmeni with beaten egg white.

Bring a large pot full of salted water to boil, you also can use chicken or meat broth. Without crowding, drop the pelmeni into the boiling water (or broth), stirring to prevent sticking, until the pelmeni comes to surface (about 4 minutes). Remove the pelmeni and put them on a large plate.

Melt butter over medium heat and drizzle it over the pelmeni.

You can also serve pelmeni with sour cream or a white sauce. The children like them with ketchup.

POTATO FRITTERS (LUXEMBOURG)

There can be no doubt that the Grand-Duchy of Luxembourg is truly a gastronomer's delight. Most traditional dishes are of peasant origin, but Luxembourg's affinities with both French and German culture have long ago been translated into the country's speciality foods. Potato Fritters (Gromperekichelcher) are some of the more succulent traditional snacks.

Ingredients:

* 1 kg potatoes
* 3 onions
* 2 shallots
* Parsley
* 4-6 eggs
* 2 tablespoons flour
* Salt
* Pepper
* Oil for frying

Directions:

Wash, peel and coarsely grate the potatoes. Put them in a cloth and press them.

Chop the parsley, shallots, and onions, and mix them in. Add the beaten eggs. Salt and pepper to taste. Prepare with the flour.

Heat the oil in a pan until very hot. Form flat cakes out of the potato mixture and fry them in the oil until golden brown on both sides.

PAN ROASTED SALMON (ICELAND)

Iceland is a haven of fishing grounds. Seventy percent of its export earnings come from its marine products. Marine products are abundant in Iceland so it's no wonder that fish places prominently in Icelandic diets. Second to fish consumption, meat, particularly Lamb, is part of Icelandic diet. Salmon is abundant from May to September. Thus, poached, fried, smoked, grilled and pickled salmon are regular fares in Icelandic tables during these months. Served on seared poblano and red peppers with manila mango, ginger, lime coulees, pan roasted salmon is a popular Icelandic snack.

Ingredients

* 7 oz wild troll king salmon fillets
* 1 manila mango
* 1/4 tsp fresh ginger, finely chopped
* 1oz fresh lime juice
* 1oz water
* 1 tspoon honey
* 1 Poblano chile
* 1/2 red bell pepper
* 1/4 tsp garlic
* 1/2 tsp soy sauce
* salt & pepper
* 1tbs canola oil

Directions

Remove skin and seeds from mango, extracting as much pulp and juice as possible. Place in blender, add lime juice, water, honey, and ginger. Process until smooth.

Remove seed and pith from peppers. Slice on the bias into 1/2 inch strips. Sear in 1/2 tbs of hot oil until slightly charred and tender. Add garlic and soy sauce, continue cooking until dry.

In a hot pan add remaining oil. Season with salt and pepper. Add, salmon fillets, cut side down, and sear until light brown. Turn and place in 450° oven until done (approx. six minutes).

BANITSA WITH SPINACH (BULGARIA)

Bulgaria is full of vegetable plots and orchards, and fresh fruit and vegetables are half the secret of Bulgarian food. The most common Bulgarian snack food is banitsa (often referred to by its diminutive form, banichka, or known in some areas as byurek), a flaky pastry filled with cheese or spinach, on occasion, meat. At its best, the banitsa is a delicious light bite. Banitsa can be served as either appetizer or snack, depending on the filling. Other important Bulgarian snack ingredients and recipes are pita, which is similar to the bread and is used for sandwiches, Mekitsas, round bread loaves with cheese and ears. Ears do not include any animal meat, although they bear this name. The name was given because of the shape. The ingredients that are used to prepare ears are: yeast, flour, butter, sheep cheese and salt. Despite the fact that a low number of ingredients are used to prepare recipes such as this one, the snacks are very appreciated, all over the country.

Ingredients

* 1 kg flour,
* 1 kg spinach,
* white Cheese,
* 3/2 cupful of yogurt,
* 200g butter,
* 1 spoonful sunflower oil,
* 1 spoonful vinegar,
* salt

Directions

1. Cook the cleaned and finely cut spinach in some of the butter.
2. After having cooled, stir in crumbled Cheese and yoghurt.
3. Knead a hard dough from the flour, oil, vinegar, salt and water.
4. Roll into five sheets (1 kg of ready rolled pastry sheets may also be used).
5. Line a baking dish with butter, place 1 sheet on the bottom and top with the spinach filling.
6. Add a second sheet, filling and so on.
7. Bake in a moderate oven.

CROATIAN BOW KNOTS (CROATIA)

The traditional dishes that are prepared by the Croatians have very old origins. The Croatian dishes are mostly based on meat. The Turkish influence is felt in the great amounts of spices that are used, meat that is enhanced with onions and loaded with garlic. Austrians affected the Croatian cuisine and the influence can be seen in dishes that contain cabbage and in breaded dishes or desserts that is served at the breakfast. It is made of cheese, fish and bread. The dairy products also are important for the Croatians. such as: strudel, donuts, cream puffs and cakes that contain walnut cream. Croatian Bow Knots (Hrostule) are always a favorite treat. They are easy to make and often whipped up when unexpected guests arrive. Children in particular love these.

Ingredients

* 2 eggs
* 2 tbsps Sugar
* 1 tsp melted butter
* 2 cups flour
* 1/2 cup milk
* 1/2 tsp salt

Directions

Mix eggs and Sugar together and add melted butter and salt. Add flour and milk; mix well. Roll out thin as for noodles and then cut into very thin 1" x 6" strips and fold them into a knot before frying. Deep fry in hot vegetable oil and when lightly brown (they should start rising to the top at this point) remove them to a platter and sprinkle generously with powdered sugar.

POTATO DUMPLINGS (CZECH REPUBLIC)

In-between meals, Czech people are used to eating snacks, some as quick as a sandwich, and others prepared hot as side dishes for other meals. Sandwiches usually have cheese and ham in their composition, mayonnaise, and sometimes ketchup and mustard. Fresh tomatoes or cucumbers will only be used during summertime for the making of a sandwich. Smažený sýr, basically fried cheese in bread crumbs is great as a snack, as well as Potato Dumplings (Bramborove Knedliky), that can be served as side dishes as well.

Ingredients

* 2 lbs potatoes
* 8 tablespoons farina (cream of wheat)
* 10 tablespoons flour
* 1 tablespoon salt
* 1 egg

Directions

1. Boil potatoes, then peel and mash.
2. Add farina, flour, salt and egg.
3. Work dough well.
4. Divide into dumplings.
5. Place into boiling water, cook for 20 minutes.

Serve warm with cilantro chutney or a dip of your choice

BOREK (CYPRUS)

Cypriot cuisine is shaped by the island's Mediterranean climate, its geography and history. Reflecting the two dominant populations, Cypriot cuisine has evolved as a fusion of Greek and Turkish cuisine with local twists to well known dishes. Further influences are evident from neighboring countries, namely Arabic and Middle Eastern cuisine. Cypriot people celebrate meals and eat without rush all day long. Between the meals they usually eat nuts and almonds roasted or covered with different delicacies (Soushoúkou—almonds in the icing made of molasses and rosy water which can be found almost everywhere), fruit and pastries. Among the last ones the most popular are those filled with olives, dumplings with sesame filling or dumplings made of pumpkin with raisins. Stuffed baked goods in the South include eliopitta, olive-turnover; tashinopitta, a pastry with sesame paste; and kolokotes, a triangular pastry stuffed with pumpkin, cracked wheat and raisins. In the North, street vendors offer Borek, a rich, flaky layered pastry contain-ing bits of meat or cheese.

Ingredients (serves 4):

Main:

- —454 gr. (1 lb) Filo Pastry
- —50 ml extra virgin olive oil
- —2/3 cup milk
- —1/2 cup water
- —2 eggs
- —1 tsp salt
- —3L (13 x 9 x 2") Pyrex casserole dish

Spinach Filling

—1 pkg. (300 gr. frozen chopped spinach
—1/4 cup crumbled feta
—1 onion, chopped
—1 tbsp extra virgin olive oil
—Salt
Black pepper

Directions

Put the salt, pepper, olive oil and onion in a pan. Cook on medium heat for two minutes. Add the spinach and continue cooking until all liquid has evaporated. Put aside and add the feta cheese.

Now we can move on to the main ingredients. In a bowl, mix the eggs, olive oil, milk and water with a whisk. This liquid mix will go between every two layers of the pastry, and will complement filling. The spinach filling will go in the middle only.

Grease the casserole dish. Place two sheets of the pastry in the bottom and over the sides of the dish. Spread 2-3 tablespoons of the liquid mix on top. Take another two sheets of pastry, fold in half, and stack in the dish. Continue layering until halfway through the pastry. Then, spread all of your main filling onto the stack. Resume layering the pastry and the liquid mix until the pastry is finished. Then, fold the sides of the bottom layer over. Make sure you pour the remaining mix on top to prevent burning in the oven.

Leave the casserole dish in the fridge for 2-3 hours, this way it will be more crispy and tasty. Pre-heat the oven to 175 C (350 F). Bake until golden brown, for approximately 20 minutes.

This recipe goes well with cherries on the side or Ayran. You can have it as a main dish (4 servings) or with afternoon tea as a snack.

POTATO LEFSE (NORWAY)

Norway's food customs have more to offer than the salted preserved fish of the olden days. Norwegian meals are generous, laden with a variety of delights and complemented by social coffee (kaffe) sessions in the afternoon that have become increasingly popular. Breakfast (frokost) in Norway may be served as an enormous buffet, called a koldtbord, or as a smaller selection of dairy, eggs, fish and breads. Lunch (lunsj) is often simpler and lighter than breakfast. Lunch may be a smaller smorgasbord or open-faced sandwiches of pate, cold meats or cheese served with fruit and coffee. Dinner (middag) comes early, around 4 p.m., and is usually more plain than other meals—a hearty stew or a combination of meatballs and gravy called kjøttkaker with beer or wine. Snacks may be served between lunch and dinner and just before bed (a small version koldtbord); brown cheese (geitost) on bread is one of the most typical Norwegian snacks. Potet Lafse or Potato Lafse is one popular snack that can also be served as breakfast, lunch or dinner.

POTATO LEFSE I (POTET LEFSE I)

Ingredients

> 3 large baking potatoes
> 2 T butter
> 1/4 cup (1/2 dl) heavy cream
> 1/2 tsp. sugar
> 1 tsp. salt
> 1 cup (2 1/2 dl) flour, or more

Directions

> Boil the potatoes without peeling, peel and mash while still warm and put through ricer. To get the lumps out, you might have to put them

through ricer more than once. Add the remaining ingredients, mix well, cover and chill for 8 hours or overnight. Mix in 1/2 cup flour. Divide into 15-16 balls if you want dinner-plate size. Using a grooved rolling pin with sock, (sock optional), and pastry canvas, roll each ball out as thin as possible. use flour as needed (but not too much), and keep balance of dough in the refrigerator. Bake each lefse on medium to hot griddle, turning until both sides are flecks with brown. Do not over bake.

POTATO LEFSE II (POTET LEFSE II)

Ingredients

* 4 cups (9 1/2 dl) potatoes, cooked
* 1 tsp. salt
* 1/2 cup (1 1/4 dl) whipping cream
* 1/2 cup (1 1/4 dl) Crisco oil
* 2 T Sugar
* 1 1/2 cups (3 1/2 dl) flour

Directions

* Boil potatoes, add salt, cream and oil to warm potatoes.

* Cool the potatoes before adding flour.

* Cut down a little on the cream and oil.

* Mix Sugar with flour and add, kneading as you roll them out with a grooved rolling pin.

Bake on takke, round griddle.

SWISS TWISTS (SWITZERLAND)

The food culture of Switzerland has been influenced by its neighbors, especially Italy and France. Pasta and pizza are very familiar in Switzerland. Swiss cuisine is firmly rooted in the dairy products, like cheese, milk, cream, butter and/or yoghurt. Almost anything that you want to prepare in a Swiss way has to contain more or less dairy products. Let your tongue taste the somewhat different twist in this Swiss Twists! Yes, here's a simple, yet different recipe for your favorite Swiss Twists. Try it and relish!

Ingredients

1 cup light cream
2 eggs, well beaten
1/4 teaspoon salt
2 cups sifted flour
1/2 cup butter
Sugar

Directions

Combine cream, eggs and salt and mix well.

Add flour to make a soft dough.

Turn onto a lightly floured board, dot with butter and work into the dough.

Butter should be firm but not hard.

Place dough in refrigerator several hours.

Roll out on a lightly floured board about 1/8 inch thick.

Cut into diamond or oblong shapes.

Slash each cookie through the center with 1/2-inch gash.

Fry in deep hot fat (375°F.) until browned.

Drain on absorbent paper.

Roll in granulated sugar while hot.

SWEDISH PANCAKES (SWEDEN)

Swedish food is usually simple and considered as healthy. One can eat lots of kinds of food in Sweden.

Sweden's cuisine is based on a simple cooking style, often very mild and not very spicy. The meals are not very elaborate and many will find them scarce in vegetables. Traditional recipes were influenced by the lack of plants due to the long Swedish winters and many modern dishes still include only small amounts of vegetables. rutabaga is a native turnip that was among the most popular plant types in Swedish cooking until it got replaced by the Potato. Swedish cuisine uses elements from various cooking traditions borrowed from their neighbors and developed from their own traditional dishes. Swedish Pancakes belong to this category.

Ingredients

* 3 eggs
* 2½ cups low-fat milk
* 1¼ cups flour
* ½ teaspoon salt
3 tablespoons butter, melted

Directions

1. Beat the eggs with half the milk.
2. Beat in flour and salt.
3. Stir in melted butter and remaining milk.
4. Heat a griddle with vegetable oil.
5. Pour about ¼ cup batter onto the griddle and cook over medium heat 1 to 2 minutes.
6. Turn the pancakes and cook about ½ minute.
7. Serve immediately.

CHICKEN KIEV (RUSSIA / UKRAINE)

One of the most famous Russian dishes, Chicken Kiev, without any doubts belong to the row of culinary masterpieces. It deserves its name both—the way it looks and the way it tastes. Classical "Kotlety-po-Kievsky" was invented in the earlier 20th century in St. Petersburg. It is a dish of boneless chicken breast pounded and rolled around cold unsalted butter, then breaded and fried. It is also known as Chicken Supreme. As its popularity has spread internationally, various seasonings have been added to the butter, most commonly garlic. A real one has to be juicy.

Ingredients

1/3 cup unsalted butter
1 tablespoon lemon juice
Freshly ground white pepper, to taste
4 whole chicken breasts, skinned, boned and halved
3 tablespoons all purpose flour
2 small eggs beaten
1-1/2 cups dry bread crumbs
Vegetable oil for frying

Method

Blend together the butter, lemon juice and pepper. Roll the mixture and cover with plastic wrap. Chill for several hours or until quite hard.

Pound the chicken breasts gently between two sheets of wax (greaseproof) paper, to flatten without ripping the meat. Place a roll of butter in the center of each fillet, turn in the ends and roll up firmly, ensuring there are no tears in the meat through which butter could seep out.

Dip the rolls lightly in the flour, shaking off any excess. Dip into the beaten egg, then roll in the bread crumbs until well coated. Cover and chill for several hours.

Add the oil to a deep fryer, to a depth of 2-3 inch. When the oil is hot, drop the rolls in batches, allowing plenty of room in the deep fryer. Fry until they are deep golden brown, about 8-10 minutes.

Place on paper towels and keep warm in a low oven until the rest of the chicken is fried.

Serve immediately—it is essential that this dish be served piping hot.

CABBAGE ROLLS (FINLAND)

Due to the harsh climate, traditional Finnish cuisine included many grains and berries. Today contemporary Finns enjoy a wide variety of modern foods typical of Western Europe. Hunting and fishing are popular in Finland, with fish, moose and deer plentiful. The Finnish diet combines traditional country fare and upper class cuisine with modern continental style cooking. Spices have been adopted from both East and West. Kaalikaaryleet or Cabbage Rolls is a popular gourmet snack in Finland.

Ingredients

A large cabbage
Water, Salt

Filling:

1/2 cups raw rice
Water, salt
300 g ground meat
The core of the cabbage
1 small onion, grated
1/4 cup (1/2 dl) dried breadcrumbs
1/4 cup (1/2 dl) water
1/4 cup (1/2 dl) cream salt, black pepper

For frying:

Butter,
Margarine, or oil

On top:

2 tbsp syrup

Directions

1. Cut out the core of the cabbage.
2. Cook the cabbage in salted water until done.
3. Remove the leaves and drain. Pare down the thick base of each leaf.
4. Cook the rice in salted water.
5. Let the breadcrumbs swell in the water and cream mixture.
6. Mix the ground meat, bread-crumbs, onion, seasonings, and rice. Dice the core of the cabbage. And add to the ground meat mixture. Season.
7. Spread cabbage leaves on a board. Put 1-2 tablespoons of filling on each leaf. Wrap into little packages.
8. Place the packages side by side in a greased baking dish. Top with a few dabs of butter and pour on syrup.
9. Bake at 425 degrees F (225 degrees C) until slightly brown. Turn and bake some more.
10. Lower the temperature to 350 degrees F (180 degrees C). Baste and bake for 45-60 minutes.
11. Serve with cranberry jam or fresh puréed berries.

CRUMPETS (SCOTLAND)

These are soft pancake-like fare but made larger and more thinly than pancakes. They can be spread with butter and/or jam and they are traditionally rolled up before eating. The quantities below will make about 16 crumpets

Ingredients:

8 oz plain flour (2 cups all purpose flour)
2 tablespoons caster sugar/fine granulated sugar
Pinch of salt
2 large eggs, separated into whites and yolks
2 tablespoons melted butter
15 oz milk

Method:

Beat the egg yolks and blend in the sifted flour, sugar, salt. Then add in the melted butter and milk to make a thin batter about the consistency of thin cream. Beat the egg whites to the soft peak stage and quickly add to the batter, folding with a knife or metal spoon.

Heat a lightly greased griddle or a frying pan and pour in large spoonfuls of the batter. Each crumpet should spread thinly to about 4/5" in diameter and you may have to roll the pan to achieve this. When the batter is brown underneath and slightly bubbly on top, turn and cook on the other side. Keep them warm by stacking on a clean tea towel and eat soon after.

MAMALIGA BALLS (ROMANIA)

Romanian Mamaliga Balls are another example of Eastern Europeans' love of food tucked inside other food. Cornmeal porridge—mamaliga—is cooked until thick, portioned into balls and stuffed with salami or smoked sausage and fried. The influence of the Mediterranean on Romanian cuisine is evidenced in this cornmeal porridge which is the equivalent of Italian polenta. This is a great appetizer, snack or finger food appropriate with cocktails. You can substitute the salami with chunks of ham or cheese.

Ingredients:

* 2 cups fine yellow cornmeal
* 2 1/2 cups water
* 3/4 teaspoon salt
* 1 tablespoon butter
* 1 cup salami or smoked sausage or pepperoni, casing removed and roughly chopped

Preparation:

1. Stir cornmeal, water and salt together in a heavy saucepan. Bring to a boil, reduce heat and, stirring frequently, cook 12 minutes or until thick enough to be scooped. Stir in butter and adjust seasonings.
2. Heat oil in a heavy-bottomed pot or deep fryer to 350 degrees. Using a cookie scoop, portion out balls. Flatten mamaliga in the palm of your hand, add a chunk of salami to the center, seal completely and roll into a ball.
3. Fry balls 2-3 minutes or until golden brown. Drain on paper towels. Serve warm with sliced tomatoes and fresh herbs or a dipping sauce of your choice.

KOPYTKA (POLAND)

The dish is a part of Belarusian, Lithuanian and Polish cuisine. Although it reminds Italian gnocchi, Kopytka, also called 'Little Hooves' are served in a different way—with onion, bacon or . . . sugar. Of course one can add variety of ways of eating those potato dumplings that remind with their shape little hooves. This is actually what the name 'KOPYTKA' derives from as it is a Polish word for hooves.

Ingredients:

Potatoes (about 5 medium sized)
Flour (about a cup and a half but probably more)
1 egg

For topping

Breadcrumbs (1/2 cup)
Butter (3 tbsp)

Directions

1. Peel and boil potatoes until cooked and tender.
2. Mash thoroughly and leave to go cold.
3. Add egg and add some flour, start to mix it all and add more and more flour until all the dough is not sticky to touch.
4. Flour a large board and roll out the dough into a snake shape about an inch high and thick.
5. Cut into diamond shapes that resemble hooves (otherwise it's not truly kopytka).
6. Boil a large pot of salted water with a little oil

7. Add kopytka (do not overcrowd pot).
8. After they start to float, give them extra few minutes then remove to strain
9. Add topping of your choice

Topping:

Fry breadcrumbs in melted butter until golden. It should be moist yet crumbly.

DUTCH PANCAKE CHICKEN (NETHERLANDS)

Dutch pancakes are as big as a dinner plate and in the old days even bigger (12"/30cm). Nowadays you may find such big pancakes on the menu of a restaurant, but at home they make them the dinner plate size. They are either eaten as a savory (with smoked sausage or bacon and cheese) or as a sweet (plain with golden (or maple) syrup or with apples, or sugar). In Holland there are many 'pancake restaurants' which serve pancakes only. Some even offering over 20 different types from pancakes with cherries and whipped cream or with chopped mush-rooms, bacon and assorted vegetables. Dutch Pancake Chicken is one of the most popular varities of pancakes.

Ingredients

* 1 (9 ounce.) pkg. frzn green beans
* 2 whole lg. chicken breasts
* 1 tbs. cooking or possibly dry sherry
* 2 teaspoon cornstarch
* 3 tbsp. salad oil
* 1 med. sized onion, sliced
* 1 (6 ounce.) jar marinated artichoke hearts
* 1/4 c. water
* 1 1/2 teaspoon chicken flavor instant bouillon
* 1/2 teaspoon salt
* 1 med. sized tomato, cut into wedges
* 1/2 (8 ounce.) pkg. Mozzarella cheese, shredded (1 c.)

Directions

1. Prepare green beans as label directs; drain. Remove skin and bones from chicken breasts; cut chicken breasts into 1/4" wide strips. Place chicken in bowl with Worcestershire sauce, sherry and cornstarch; mix well. Set aside.

2. Prepare Dutch pancakes (Directions follow at No.6).

3. Meanwhile, in 5 qt oven over medium heat, in warm salad oil, cook onion till tender, stirring occasionally. With slotted spoon, remove onion to plate.

4. In oil remaining in Dutch oven over high heat, cook chicken mix just till chicken loses its pink color and is tender, about 2 to 3 min. Reduce heat to medium. Return onion to oven; add in green beans, artichoke hearts with their marinade, water, bouillon and salt; cook, stirring constantly, till mix is heated through and thickens slightly. Add in tomato wedges; keep hot till pancake is ready.

5. Without removing skillet with pancake from oven, carefully spoon chicken mix onto pancake. Sprinkle with cheese. Bake 2 to 3 min till cheese melts. Serve immediately.

6. DUTCH PANCAKES: Preheat oven to 425 degrees. In small bowl with mixer at low speed, beat 4 Large eggs, 2/3 c. all-purpose flour, 2/3 c. lowfat milk and 1/2 tsp. salt till smooth. In oven safe 12" skillet, place 1 Tbs. butter. Place skillet in oven till butter melts; remove from oven, tilting skillet so butter coats the bottom and sides. Pour batter into skillet. Bake about 15 min till pancake is puffed and golden.

IRISH SAUSAGE KEBABS (IRELAND)

Irish sausage kebabs are a type of sandwich, similar to an American hot dog, that are served in most fast food restaurants in Ireland. They consist of an Irish sausage, topped with tomatoes and onions, that have been marinated in vinaigrette, then wrapped in puff pastry and baked until browned and heated through. Kebabs are not to be confused with Middle Eastern Kabobs, or Shish Kabobs, which are totally different.

Ingredients

2 1 lb. packages Donnelly Irish Sausages
2 tomatoes, diced to 1/4 inch
1 medium onion, diced to 1/4 inch
1-1/2 c. vinaigrette marinade or salad dressing
1/4 tsp. ground curry powder
1/4 tsp. ground ginger
1 package ready-made puff pastry thawed (2 sheets)
1 beaten egg

Method

Start one day ahead. Marinate the onion and tomatoes in the refrigerator overnight. The next day, fry the sausages until thoroughly cooked; drain and set aside. Spread the pastry and roll lightly on a floured surface. Cut into 4-inch squares. Place one teaspoonful marinated vegetables in the center, then place one sausage on top.

Wrap and seal the seam with a little water, placing them on an ungreased baking sheet, seam side down. Brush with beaten egg and bake 12 to 15 minutes until pastry is risen, cooked through and golden brown. Serve warm as an appetizer.

PALACSINTA (HUNGARY)

The best-known ingredient in Hungarian food is the red-powdered spice called paprika. It is used to flavor many dishes. Other staples of Hungarian cooking include onions, cabbage, potatoes, noodles, and caraway seeds. Both cream and sour cream are used heavily in Hungarian food. Dumplings (dough wrapped around different kinds of fillings) are very popular as are cabbages or green peppers stuffed with meat and rice. Another favorite is the pancake called Palacsinta. It is often rolled or wrapped around different kinds of fillings.

Ingredients

4 eggs
1/2 cup milk or light cream
1/2 tsp. salt
1 tsp. sugar
1 cup flour
1/2 tsp. vanilla extract
Confectioners' sugar
4 tbs. oil
Jams (such as strawberry, raspberry, apricot, peach, plum, blackberry, etc.)

Directions

In a medium bowl, whisk together the eggs and milk. Whisk in the salt, granulated sugar, vanilla. Add flour slowly constantly whisking until mixture has a thickness that can be described as coating the spoon. Add more flour if necessary until you have this thickness. Set aside for 30 minutes.

Put the oil in a soup bowl and use the back of a large soupspoon to apply when cooking.

Take a nonstick 10-inch skillet and add 1½ tsp. of oil to the skillet, coat base of skillet while heating until very hot. When the oil shimmers pour or ladle in about 1/8 cup (2-3 tbs.) of batter. Remember to use as little batter as possible to coat the skillet. Palacsintas are supposed to be very thin. Using your arm in a circular motion to swirl the pan so the batter coats the bottom of the pan. This is a trick that you will get use to doing. If the batter leaves holes in the batter, just ladle a little batter to cover the holes. Replace the pan on the burner and cook just until set and bubbles begin to form and the underside is lightly browned. [At this stage don't forget to apply a little oil using the back of your pre-oiled soupspoon.]

Using a knife or spatula, flip and cook until the other side is lightly browned. Transfer to the warmed platter. Repeat until the batter is used up. Remove the palacsinta's (crepes) from the oven. One by one, spread each crepe with a thin layer of jam and roll up like a cigar.

Place 2 rolled crepes on each of 4 serving plates. Sprinkle with confectioners' sugar and serve.

WITLOF-BITES (BELGIUM)

Witlof (Belgian endive), Goat's Cheese & Bacon Bites as a popular Belgian starter or a party snack. This is really the kind of dish that you just assemble as needed, so a recipe with rigid amounts seems rather forced here. It's all about frying off some bacon, cutting up a little endive, and assembling with a bit of cut or crumbled goat's cheese, nuts and some herbs. Nothing fancy, but oh so tasty!

Ingredients:

* Witlof (Belgian endive)
* Bacon rashers
* Soft Goat's cheese
* Halved (shelled) walnuts
* Celery Leaf or Flat Leaf Parsley
* Lemon juice
* Salt & Pepper

Preparation:

Cut the stalky end off the witlof to seperate the leaves. Now rinse under running water and drain. Pat the leaves dry gently. Assemble on a serving dish. In a dry non-stick frying pan, fry the bacon rashers until crispy. Drain on paper towels. Cut some goat's cheese into small squares or crumble. Top the small indentation at the bottom of each witlof leaf with a bit of goat's cheese, a bacon shard, a walnut half and a small sprig of herb. Now season, drizzle some lemon juice over the plate and serve.

Tips:

Use goat's cheese for this that has not only been marinated in oil, but has been infused with herbs or chili.

SWEDISH BAKED POTATOES (SWEDEN)

In Sweden, snacks may range from chips and crackers to nutritious sandwiches. Swedish Baked Potatoes are popular snacks in all Scandinavian countries. Cheez doodles—delicate and crispy corn arches, with mild cheese flavor, grilled potato chips—crispy potato chips flavored with onion or dill chips—potato chips flavored with dill are other quite popular snacks all around Sweden. Light sandwiches with some thin meat and dill may also serve as a popular snack. Although they are not traditional Swedish snacks, peanuts and other types of nuts are well known and appreciated.

Ingredients

* 8 medium potatoes, peeled
* 1 1/2 ounces butter, melted
* 3 cloves garlic, crushed
* 1 1/2 teaspoons salt
* pepper
1 1/2 ounces Parmesan cheese

Directions

* Cut the potatoes into thin slices 3/4 way through.

* Put half of the butter and garlic in an oven and place the potatoes in the dish.

* Sprinkle with salt, pepper.

* Drizzle with remaining butter and garlic.

* Bake in 375f oven.

* Baste with the butter in the dish.

* After 30 minutes sprinkle with the Cheese and bread crumbs.

* Finish baking—potatoes should be done and golden.

PURPLE POTATO LUTKE (BELARUS)

It is the national dish of Belarus. Latkes or Potato pancakes, are shallow-fried pancakes of grated potato and egg, often flavored with grated onion and may be herbs. The purple potatoes are high in anthocyanins—the pigments that impart the vibrant colors to the fruits and vegetables. Like in blueberries, their antioxidant properties are known to fight cancer, and various other illnesses. When selecting, choose those that are firm and plump, avoiding those that have shriveled skins, sprouting eyes, soft spots, blemishes and green spots.

Ingredients:

1. 3-4 Large Purple Potatoes
2. 1 Large Onion
3. 1 Egg
4. 1/4 Cup Flour
5. Sea Salt
6. Black Pepper
7. Chopped Parsley (Optional)
   Oil for Frying

Preparation:

Peel and finely grate the potatoes with a box grater or food processor. Put them into cold water, then drain them in a colander and squeeze them as dry as you can by pressing them with your hands.

Put the grated potatoes in a cheese cloth (or a few layers of paper towels), pull the sides up on to the top like a pouch and squeeze out as much water as you can. If you don't drain and squeeze them dry, they might get runny during frying and finally the latkes will get soggy.

Grate the onions; drain them and squeeze the water out in the same way as you did with the potatoes.

Mix the potatoes, onions, and chopped parsley.

Beat the eggs lightly with salt and pepper; add to the potatoes mix. Add the flour and stir to combine well.

Heat about 1/4 inch of oil in cast iron skillet. Take spoonfuls of the mixture and drop into the hot oil. Flatten them with the back of the spoon, and lower the heat so that the fritters cook through evenly. When one side is brown, turn over and brown the other.

Lift out and place them on paper towels.

Serve very hot with applesauce, sour cream or your favorite condiment.

FRUIT PIZZA (AUSTRIA)

Lunch is traditionally the main meal of the day in Austria and most people have only smaller meals for dinner (light meals, sandwiches, essentially things you would have for lunch in the Anglo-American sphere). Snacks and fast food are common (like in all countries) and often regionally distinct. The most popular snack, especially as lunch snack for school children, is Fruit Pizza.

Ingtrdients

Topping:

> 1 cup (250 g) cream cheese
> 1 Tbsp (15 ml) honey
> 1 Tbsp (15 ml) lemon juice
> 1 banana
> 3 kiwis
> Cluster of red grapes or in-season fruit
> 2 Tbsp (30 ml) apricot or peach jam
> 1 Tbsp (15 ml) water

Pizza dough:

> 2/3 cup (165 ml) butter
> 1 cup (250 ml) honey
> 1 free-range egg
> 1 1/2 tsp (7 ml) pure almond extract
> 1 1/2 cup (375 ml) whole wheat flour
> 1 1/2 tsp (7 ml) baking powder
> 1/4 tsp (1 ml) salt
> Butter, to grease pan

Directions:

To make the pizza crust: Heat oven to 350°F (180°C). Grease a pizza stone (or flat bottom of a springform pan) with butter, using wax paper to spread the butter.

Using a hand mixer, mix cream butter and honey in a mixing bowl. Add egg and beat until smooth. Mix in the almond extract. In a separate bowl, mix flour with baking powder and salt. Add flour mixture to butter-honey mixture, then knead with hands to a smooth dough. Spread pizza dough onto greased pizza pan and bake in the oven for 12 to 15 minutes until slightly browned. Remove from oven and cool.

To make the topping: Place cream cheese, honey and lemon juice in a mixing bowl. Using a hand mixer, cream them to a smooth spread. Cover pizza crust with the spread. Peel and slice the banana and kiwis. Decorate the pizza crust with the banana, kiwi and grapes (or other seasonal fruit). In a small pot, heat apricot or peach jam with water until jam dissolves, stirring with a wooden spoon. Using a pastry brush, lightly brush this mixture over fruit. This prevents the fruit from becoming brown and unappetizing.

BOREK (TURKEY)

Borek is one of the most popular pastries in Turkish cuisine. Börek (also burek, boereg, and other variants on the name) is a kind of pie popular throughout the former Ottoman Empire. It's similar to pastry but made with phyllo pastry. You can put any ingredient you like. There are a lot of kinds of borek; with cheese, with potatoes, with minced meat, with spinach, with green lentil, with leek, etc. It's so easy and delicious. You can have it with your breakfast or at 5 o'clock tea or at any time you like. The top of the börek is often sprinkled with sesame seeds.

Ingredients:

For dough:

* 2 eggs (one of the egg yolks is for topping)
* 1 teaspoon salt
* 1\3 cups olive oil plus 1 tablespoon for topping
* 2\3 cup whole milk
* 1 1\2 teaspoon baking powder
* flour (almost 4 cups)

For filling:

* 1 packet baby spinach (chopped small pieces)
* 1 big chopped onion
* 1 pinch salt and pepper
* 1 packet blue cheese (*my contribution)
* 2-3 tablespoon olive oil

Method:

Lightly grease a round 27 cm (10 inch) cake pan with olive oil

Preheat oven 350F

In a large pan, cook the onion with olive oil until it turns yellow. Add the spinach, cook until spinach dries down and add the salt and pepper. You can also use meat and potatoes for filling.

Next, in a large bowl, add all the ingredients but with only 1 cup flour. Start kneading. It should be very sticky, add flour one cup at a time and continue kneading until dough becomes soft and not sticky. Stop adding flour.

Dust the work surface with some flour. Make small balls from dough and roll each ball very thin 8 inch diameter. (or little longer and narrower)

Pour 2 or 3 tablespoons filling and 1 tablespoon blue cheese one side of dough and make a tight roll. Make a ring and put it in the middle of the pan. And than start wrapping the roll from middle to out. Brush the Borek with the egg yolk and olive oil, bake it until brown. Serve when it is almost hot.

LABDA (GEORGIA)

The Georgian cuisine is very specific to the country, but also contains some influences from the Middle Eastern and European culinary traditions. Georgian people are famous for their hospitality. They respect guests and are good at being friendly and generous while entertaining them, especially in their own home. The cuisine offers a variety of dishes, high in various herbs and spices. The food, in addition to various meat dishes, also offers a variety of vegetarian meals. The cuisine is very varied with different dishes cooked daily. Labda—the most popular variety, is basically potato pancake. This large, rich pancake makes a quick and filling supper any time of the year.

Ingredients:

1 pound of boiling potatoes
1 cup of finely chopped walnuts
2 tablespoons of finely chopped parsley
1/2 teaspoon of salt
Freshly ground black pepper
3 large eggs, beaten
2 tablespoons of butter
2 tablespoons of corn oil

Instructions:

Boil the potatoes until tender; peel and mash them. Stir in the walnuts, parsley, salt, pepper to taste and eggs, mixing them well.

In a 10-inch skillet with sloping sides, melt 1 tablespoon each of butter and oil. When hot, spoon the pancake batter into the pan, pressing down with a spatula to form and even pancake. Cook over medium high heat for about 4 minutes, or until the bottom of the pancake is brown and crusty. Slide the pancake onto a platter. Melt the remaining butter and oil in the skillet, then invert the pancake into the skillet and fry the other side until brown, about 4 minutes more. Slide onto a platter and serve, cut into wedges.

THE CONTINENT OF AFRICA

African cuisine is a generalized term collectively referring to the cuisines of Africa. The continent of Africa is the second largest land-mass on Earth, and is home to hundreds of different cultural and ethnic groups. This diversity is also reflected in the many local culinary traditions in terms of choice of ingredients, style of preparation and cooking techniques.

Traditionally, the various cuisines of Africa use a combination of locally available fruits, cereal grains and vegetables, as well as milk and meat products. In some parts of the continent, the traditional diet features a preponderance of milk, curd and whey products. In much of Tropical Africa, however, cow's milk is rare and cannot be produced locally (owing to various diseases that affect livestock). Depending on the region, there are also sometimes quite significant differences in the eating and drinking habits and proclivities throughout the continent's many populations: Central Africa, East Africa, the Horn of Africa, North Africa, Southern Africa and West Africa each have their own distinctive dishes, preparation techniques, and consumption mores.

Central Africa stretches from the Tibesti Mountains in the north to vast rainforest basin of the Congo River. Central African cooking has remained mostly traditional. Nevertheless, like other parts of Africa, Central African cuisine also presents an array of dishes. The basic ingredients are plantains and cassava. Fufu-like starchy foods (usually made from fermented cassava roots) are served with grilled meat and sauces. A variety of local ingredients are used while preparing other dishes like spinach stew, cooked with tomato, peppers, chiles, onions, and peanut butter. Cassava plants are also consumed as cooked greens. Groundnut (peanut) stew is also prepared, containing chicken, okra, ginger, and other spices. Another favorite is Bambara, a porridge of rice, peanut butter and sugar. Beef and chicken are favorite meat dishes.

The cuisine of East Africa varies from area to area. In the inland savannah, the traditional cuisine of cattle-keeping peoples is distinctive in that meat products are generally absent. Cattle, sheep and goats were regarded as a form of currency and a store of wealth, and are not generally consumed as food. Maize (corn) is the basis of ugali, the East African version of West Africa's fufu. Ugali is a starch dish eaten with meats or stews. In Uganda, steamed, green bananas called matoke provide the starch filler of many meals. Around 1000 years ago, the Arabs settled in the coastal areas of East Africa, and Arabic influences are especially reflected in the Swahili cuisine of the coast—steamed cooked rice with spices in Persian style, use of saffron, cloves, cinnamon and several other spices, and pomegranate juice. Several centuries later, the British and the Indians came, and both brought with them their foods, like Indian spiced vegetable curries, lentil soups, chapattis and a variety of pickles. Just before the British and the Indians, the Portuguese had introduced techniques of roasting and marinating, as also use of spices turning the bland diet into aromatic stewed dishes. Portuguese also brought from their Asian colonies fruits like the orange, lemon and lime. From their colonies in the New World, Portuguese also brought exotic items like chilies, peppers, maize, tomatoes, pineapple, bananas, and the domestic pig—now, all these are common elements of East African foods.

North Africa lies along the Mediterranean Sea and encompasses within its fold several nations, including Morocco, Algeria, Libya, Tunisia, Mauritania, and Egypt. The roots to North African cuisine can be traced back to the ancient empires of North Africa, particularly in Egypt where many of the country's dishes and culinary traditions date back to ancient Egypt. Over several centuries traders, travelers, invaders, migrants and immigrants all have influenced the cuisine of North Africa. From the 7th century onwards, the Arabs introduced a variety of spices, like saffron, nutmeg, cinnamon, ginger and cloves, which contributed and influenced the culinary culture of North Africa. The Ottoman Turks brought sweet pastries and other bakery products, and from the New World, North Africa got potatoes, tomatoes, zucchini and chilies. Most of the North African countries have several similar dishes, sometimes almost the same dish with a different name, sometimes with a slight change in ingredients and cooking style. There are noticeable differences between the cooking styles of different nations—there's the sophisticated, full-bodied flavours of Moroccan palace cookery, the fiery dishes of Tunisian cuisine, and the humbler, simpler cuisines of Egypt and Algeria.

The cooking of Southern Africa is sometimes called 'rainbow cuisine', as the food in this region is a blend of many cultures—the indigenous African tribal societies, European and Asian. Milk was historically one of the most important components of the southern African diet. South Africans enjoy drinking sour milk products that are sold in the supermarket, and these products are comparable to American buttermilk, yogurt and sour cream. The basic ingredients of their food include seafood, meat products (including wild game), poultry, as well as grains, fresh fruits and vegetables.

A typical West African meal is heavy with starchy items, meat, spices and flavors. A wide array of staples are eaten across the region, mainly those of Fufu. Fufu is often made from starchy root vegetables such as yams, cocoyams, or cassava, but also from cereal grains like millet, sorghum or plantains. Rice-dishes are also widely eaten in the region, especially in the dry Sahel belt inland. The Portuguese, French and British have influenced the regional cuisines, and both chillies and tomatoes have become ubiquitous components of West African cuisines. The local cuisine and recipes of West Africa continue to remain deeply entrenched in the local customs and traditions, with ingredients like native rice (oryza glaberrima), rice, fonio, millet, sorghum, Bambara and Hausa groundnuts, blackeyed beans, brown beans, and root vegetables such as yams, cocoyams, sweet potatoes, and cassava.

SAMAK KEBAB (MOROCCO)

The cuisine of Morocco is rated among the best in the world and rightly so. There are few places where food is more carefully and artistically prepared, more delightfully served, more enjoyed than this country. When most people think of kebabs, the image of meat and vegetables on a skewer come to mind. Fish, however, makes an excellent addition to any skewer, specially when the end result is samak kebab, the famous Moroccan and Mediterranean dish. Its recipe features the finest fish marinade that really brings out the flavor of the fish while still maintaining the grilled flavor. This Moroccan cuisine is much influenced by Greek and Turkish cooking.

Ingredients

1-1/2 lb. thick white fish fillets
1/3 teaspoon saffron threads
2 tablespoons water
1 red onion finely chopped
1 garlic clove, finely chopped
¼ cup chopped Italian parsley 1 tablespoon chopped fresh cilantro leaves
¾ teaspoon sea salt, plus extra for serving
1/3 cup virgin olive oil
2 tablespoons lemon or lime juice
Italian parsley springs for garnish

Method

Soak the saffron threads in the water.

Cut the fish into 1-in cubes and place in a bowl.

Mix together the strained saffron water and the remaining ingredients, except the parsley springs.

Spoon the mixture over the fish cubes, mix thoroughly but lightly, and cover the bowl. Chill for at least 4 hours.

Press the fish cubes onto skewers and broil (grill) over hot coals or under a preheated broiler (griller). Cook for about 4 minutes on each side, or until cooked through but not dry. Spread any remaining marinade over the fish cubes.

Garnish with the parsley springs and serve with small bowls of extra sea salt and hot paprika.

ROASTED BUTTERNUT SQUASH (ZIMBABWE)

A landlocked country of south-central Africa, Zimbabwe (formerly known as Rhodesia) lies between the Zambezi River on the north and the Limpopo River on the south. The Europeans arrived in the 1850s and the British gained control of the Zimbabwe area (then called Rhodesia) until 1923. As a result, food unadorned with spices, commonly associated with British cooking, infiltrated Zimbabwean cuisine with sugar, bread, and tea. The crops, such as squash, corn, yams, pumpkins, peanuts, and mapopo (papaya), flourish during the summer and autumn months. Traditional Zimbabwe Recipes are those using ingredients available in Zimbabwe, including Roasted Butternut Squash, an easy to make popular snack.

Ingredients

* * 1 large butternut squash
* * 3 Tablespoons butter
* * Cinnamon, to taste

Procedure

1. Preheat oven to 425°F.
2. Remove the skin of the squash with a vegetable peeler, and cut into large chunks, discarding the seeds.
3. Place the chunks onto a large piece of foil and place the butter on top.
4. Bring up the edges of the foil around the squash and seal tightly.
5. Place on cookie sheet and roast for 20 to 25 minutes, or until the squash is tender and lightly browned.
6. Sprinkle cinnamon on top to taste.

BINCH AKARA (ZAMBIA)

Zambia's geographical location, an elevated plateau in south central Africa, kept it free of European and foreign influences. Because of Zambia's isolation from the rest of the world for the greater part of its history, its cuisine has stayed very traditional. The food served in Zambia nowadays is very similar to that served 1000 years ago. Snacks are very popular in Zambia and people eat them at any time during the day. The most common snacks are fruits, but there are also some recipes for cooked snacks. Many of these snack foods are deep-fried, while the typical Zambian main-course is most likely to be stewed in a pot. Binch Akara (Bean Drops) is a traditional Zambian recipe for a classic snack of deep fried black-eyed pea balls flavored with onion.

Ingredients

500g black-eyed peas
2 tsp salt
1 small onion, very finely-chopped
500ml vegetable oil

Method:

Add the dry beans to a blender along with 240ml water. Blend for 1 minute then pour the mixture into a large bowl. Add 500ml more water and stir until the skins float to the top. Remove the skins then strain in a colander, allowing the remaining skin and eyes to flow out.

Blend the beans once more, along with the onion and pepper. Pour into a bowl and stir with a wooden spoon for 2 minutes. You should have a thick mixture which you can scoop with a tablespoon. Heat the oil in a wok and when hot begin dropping tablespoons of the bean mixture into the hot oil. Fry until golden brown, drain on absorbent paper and serve along with wooden picks to pick-up the balls.

UGANDAN KABOBS (UGANDA)

Ugandan cuisine consists of traditional cooking with English, Arab and Asian (especially Indian) influences. Like the cuisines of most countries, it varies in complexity, from the most basic, a starchy filler with a sauce of beans or meat, to several-course meals served in upper-class homes and high-end restaurants. In the cuisine of Uganda you will find a few snacks, but the ones that you do find are truly very traditional in their nature. Most of the snacks are made from fresh fruits and vegetables and the traditional Ugandan staple. The Ugandan snacks are extremely delicious and they are very easy to make and the ingredients to the snacks are readily available in most food departmental stores. Ugandan Kabobs are a popular delicacy. These ground meat meatballs are seasoned with ginger, cumin, and coriander, then deep fried, and served with a dipping sauce of yogurt, jalapeno pepper, and parsley.

Ingredients:

1 cup plain yogurt
1/4 teaspoon salt
1 jalapeno pepper, seeded and minced
3 tablespoons chopped fresh parsley
3 slices whole wheat bread
3 eggs, beaten
1 tablespoon Worcestershire sauce
1 1/2 cups dried bread crumbs
1 cup French-fried onions
3 cloves garlic, minced
2 tablespoons minced fresh ginger root
1/2 teaspoon ground cumin
1/2 teaspoon coarsely crushed coriander seed
4 tablespoons chopped fresh parsley

1 jalapeno pepper, seeded and minced
2 pounds ground meat
3 cups vegetable oil for frying

Directions:

1. In a mixing bowl, mix together yogurt, salt, small jalapeno pepper, and 3 tablespoons chopped parsley. Set dipping sauce aside.
2. Soak bread slices in water for 3 minutes. Remove from water, and squeeze out excess moisture. Crumble into a large bowl. Mix in eggs and Worcestershire sauce. Mix in dried bread crumbs, fried onions, garlic, ginger, ground cumin, crushed coriander seed, 4 tablespoons parsley, and large jalapeno pepper. Add ground meat, and work in with your hands until well mixed.
3. Roll mixture into balls the size of walnuts.
4. Heat 3 cups of oil in a large, deep, heavy bottomed frying pan until piping hot, about 375 degrees F (190 degrees C). Cook meatballs a few at a time in hot oil until brown and crispy, about 3 to 4 minutes. To check for doneness, cut one in half to see if cooked through; it should be cooked in the center. Remove from oil using a slotted spoon, and place on a plate lined with paper towels to drain. Insert a toothpick into each meatball for serving and dipping. Serve hot or cold with dipping sauce.

SAMBUSA (SOMALIA)

Somalia is located in the Horn of Africa. Somali cuisine varies from region to region and is a mixture of native Somali, Ethiopian, Yemeni, Persian, Turkish, Indian and Italian influences. Breakfast (quraac) is an important meal for Somalis. who often start the day with some style of tea (shaah). The main dish is typically a pancake-like bread (canjeero) similar to Ethiopian injera but smaller and thinner. Lunch (qado) is often an elaborated main dish of rice (bariis) spiced with cumin (kamuun), cardamom (heyl), cloves (qaranfuul) and sage. Sambusa, a Somali version of the samosa, is probably the most popular form of a snack in Somalia. The Somali version is spiced with hot green pepper, and the main ingredient is often ground meat.

Ingredients

  * 1 (14 ounce) package spring roll wrappers
  * 2 tablespoons olive oil
  * 2 pounds ground meat
  * 1 leek, chopped
  * 2 teaspoons ground cumin
  * 2 teaspoons ground cardamom
  * 1 teaspoon salt
  * 1 teaspoon pepper
  * 1 small onion, finely chopped
  * 1 clove garlic, minced
  * 1 tablespoon all-purpose flour
  * 1 tablespoon water, or as needed
  * 1 quart oil for frying

Directions

1. Heat olive oil in a large skillet over medium heat. Add onions, leek and garlic, and cook, stirring until the onions are transparent. Add ground meat, and cook until about halfway done. Season with cumin, cardamom, salt and pepper. Mix well, and continue cooking until meat has browned.
2. In a small dish or cup, mix together the flour and water to make a thin paste. Using one wrapper at a time, fold into the shape of a cone. Fill the cone with the meat mixture, close the top, and seal with the paste. Repeat until wraps or filling are used up.
3. Heat the oil to 365 degrees F (170 degrees C) in a deep-fryer or deep heavy pot. There should be enough oil to submerge the wraps. Fry the Sambusa a few at a time until golden brown. Remove carefully to drain on paper towels.

GORRASSA (SUDAN)

Sudan is the widest African state, situated in the North-East Africa. The natural space of Sudan is characterized by tropical forests, steppes and savannas, but there are also a lot of lakes and rivers in the Southern areas; in this region, the fish is the most frequent meal. Sudanese cuisine has been changing and evolving gradually, but most of the dishes remain simple and natural. The most common aliments are Wheat, Beef and sheep meat, tomatoes, sesame seeds (Sudan is a great exporter of sesame) and rice. Sudanese cuisine has various influences, but none of them is dominating the regional culinary cultures. The Northern Sudan tends to have a very simple cuisine. In here, when it was a food crisis back in older times and wheat flour was the basic ingredients, people invented a dish called Gorrassa, a snack dish with sweet and salty taste.

Ingredients

* 250g of wheat flour
* 1/4 tsp baking powder
* 250ml water
* 1/2 tsp salt
* 50g Sultanas / dates (seedless)
* 125g butter
* 4 tbsp Sugar

Directions

1. Sift flour into bowl.
2. Add baking powder, salt and Sultanas / dates and stir in water until thick batter.
3. Pour ladle-full of batter onto non-stick flat frying pan and flatten out until evenly spread.
4. Fry at medium heat and flip when golden on one side.
5. Melt butter and pour onto cooked gorraasa and cover with Sugar.

PITTA SNACK (TANZANIA)

Tanzania is in Eastern Africa and it is surrounded by waters: the Indian Ocean and the range of the great African lakes: Malawi, Victoria and Tanganyika. The most common meals from the Tanzanian diet include all the local plants and fruits: rice, Wheat, corn, beans, cabbage, various nuts, bananas, mangos, pineapple and coconut, which is also consumed as milk. Tanzanian people are very friendly and hospitable people, who enjoy cooking and respect their valuable and old traditions. Because so many cereals and vegetables grow in the country, people are familiar to them and know how to use them best. The Tanzanian people carried on the traditions through their cooking and all simple culinary preparations and kept the naturalness of the aliments. The traditional Tanzanian cuisine is exotic, fresh and spiced and for the Tanzanian cooks and chefs, the most important aspect is that their food tastes fresh and natural.

Ingredients

* 1 package pita bread
* olive oil
* dry basil
* garlic powder or garlic salt
* Parmesan cheese
* ground cayenne pepper

Directions

1. Split the pita bread into two halves.
2. Score with knife, but don't cut completely through.
3. Brush lightly with olive oil, sprinkle lightly with basil, garlic powder and Cayenne ground pepper. Add Parmesan cheese.
4. Place on cookie sheet and bake at 350 degrees until golden or lightly browned.
5. Cool and break into pieces. Serve as snack or appetizer.

POULET YASSA (GUINEA-BISSAU)

Guinea-Bissau is positioned on the west coast of Africa and is bordered to the north by Senegal, the east and southeast by Guinea and west southwest by the Atlantic Ocean. Due to the fact that Guinea Bissau is a country that has ocean opening the most common dish is fresh fish but also fruits and vegetables. Cuisine of this exotic place reflects indigenous traditions, as well as influences from Arabs, Europeans, and Asians. A typical Guinea-Bissau meal is concentrated with starchy substance, light on meat and generous on fat. Another characteristic of Guinness cuisine is the hot spices, including peppers and chilies. Cooking techniques of Guinea Bissau often combine fish and meat, counting dried fish. Poulet Yassa (stir-fried chicken) is a much liked delicacy.

Ingredients

3-4 pounds chicken
6 lemons, squeezed.
2 cloves garlic, minced
6 onions, sliced in rounds
1 or 2 red peppers, or 1/4 to 1/2 tsp cayenne
4-6 tbsp oil bay leaf salt and pepper

Method

Wash and dry chicken and cut into pieces. Marinate chicken in mixture of lemon juice, onions, garlic, and 2-3 tbsp of the oil for several hours, turning occasionally as that all parts are covered. Remove chicken and grill, broil, or braise until all pieces are lightly browned on all sides. Drain onions and garlic, but retain the marinade. Use a heavy casserole, Dutch Oven, or fry chicken; saute onions and garlic in the reminaing oil until soft. Add chicken, bay leaf, peppers or cayenne, salt and pepper. Simmer until chicken is tender (1-1 1/2 hours) or bake covered in medium (325 degree) oven. Add marinade now and then so mixture remains moist. Serve as snack or over rice as main meal.

AMANDAZI (RWANDA)

Rwandan food is neither spicy nor hot. People eat simple meals made with locally grown ingredients.

Lunch and dinner may consist of boiled beans, bananas, sweet potatoes or cassava. Umutsima (a dish of cassava and corn), isombe (cassava leaves with Eggplant and spinach) and mizuzu (fried plantains) are common dishes. Dinner is the heaviest meal. Between meals, Rwandans often snack on fruits. Tropical fruits such as avocados, bananas, mangos and papaya are abundant in Rwanda. Roadside vendors in urban areas sell roasted corn and barbecued meat. Amandazi (fritters) is a popular snack that is also sold at street corners by the roadside vendors.

Ingredients

* 100 gm corn flour
* 30 gm wheat flour
* 20 gm sugar
* 1 egg
* ⅛ litre milk (approximately)
* oil for frying

Directions

1. In a bowl, mix flour and sugar.
2. Add the egg and milk and stir to form a viscous dough.
3. In a pan, heat the oil.
4. Add the dough one spoon at a time and fry until golden.
5. Place on paper towels to remove excess oil and serve hot.

DEEP-FRIED LAMB (LIBYA)

Libyan cuisine derives much from the traditions of the Mediterranean and North Africa, with an Italian influence, a legacy from the days when Libya was an Italian colony. Libyan cuisine is often referred to as "tent cookery"—tasty and healthy, but not sophisticated. In addition to dishes that consist of oil, milk, rice, vegetables, dates, semolina, and pasta products, meats are most of the times prepared in a manner that makes for easily digestible dishes. People from Libya love meat dishes, especially those consisting of lamb, and they are prepared in different ways. Deep-fried lamb is a popular dish at partiesve as main meal.

Ingredients:

6 lamb leg steaks, halved
1/2 tsp turmeric
1 garlic clove, grated
1 egg, beaten
1/2 tsp freshly-ground black pepper
1/2 tsp salt juice of 1 lemon
300g bread-crumbs oil for deep frying

Method:

Combine the lemon juice, salt and spices in a bowl then add the lamb pieces and toss to combine. Set aside to marinate for 10 minutes then remove the lamb before beating the egg in to the marinade. Return the lamb to the bowl then cover and refrigerate for 80 minutes.

When the lamb has marinated long enough heat oil in your deep fryer or to a depth of 6cm in a wok or large pan. When the oil is hot remove the lamb from the marinade and roll in the bread-crumbs to coat evenly. Add to the hot oil and fry until browned and cooked through (about 10 to 20 minutes depending on the size of the steaks and how well done you want the meat).

KUKU PAAKA (KENYA)

One delightful element about Kenya food is its diverse flavor. Kenyan cooking draws upon a variety of ethnic traditions merged with the seasonings and tastes of outside countries. Because of Kenya's long-standing relationship with foreign settlers and its colonization by the British, the taste, cooking methods and presentation of Kenyan foods have been greatly influenced by the Indians, Arabs, Europeans, and Pakistanis as well as some western countries. Kenyan food is mainly traditional and typical Kenyan cuisine is readily available in almost every Kenyan eatery. Kuku Paaka, coconut chicken, is a much loved snack which can also be taken as the main meal served with accompaniments like makate mimina, paratha, naan or rice.

INGREDIENTS:

- One three and a half pound chicken, skinned and cut into pieces
- Two green chillies, slit
- One tsp garlic paste
- One tsp ginger paste
- Three to four tomatoes, peeled and chopped
- Two to three small onions, chopped
- One pkt coconut cream
- One pint water
- Half a tsp turmeric
- Three tbsp lemon juice
- Salt to taste
- Few coriander leaves, chopped
- Five boiled eggs, shelled (optional)
- Six boiled and skinned potatoes (optional).

Method

1. Boil the chicken with half a tsp salt, garlic, ginger, ground green chillies, onions and two tomatoes until the chicken is cooked
2. In a separate saucepan put the coconut cream, one pint water, one to two tomatoes, slit green chillies, salt and a little turmeric, and bring to boil, stirring all the time.
3. Cook on high heat for fifteen to twenty minutes and then reduce heat
4. When the chicken is cooked, pour a little of the coconut cream gravy over the pieces and grill on both sides for a few minutes
5. Transfer the grilled chicken into the coconut gravy and cook for a while
6. Turn off the heat and add lemon juice
7. Add the boiled eggs and potatoes (optional)
8. Garnish with chopped coriander leaves

OVEN-FRIED FISH (GHANA)

Ghana is situated on the West coast of Central Africa and its relief is mainly a wide field and a high plateau. Ghana is a country covered in plantations and it is the third global producer of cocoa. Ghanaian people are recognized as one of the friendliest people in Africa and food is a way of expressing themselves and the relation with the others. All Ghanaian people are cooks, as food is a familiar and hospitable way of being friendly, even to strangers or tourists. There is food on the streets, as anybody is selling various meals and aliments in stands or just in wide bowls, from which they serve the customers. Fishing is a main activity in Ghana and that is why so many meals are based on fish: from soups, to snacks and main courses. Crispy oven-fried fish is Ghanians favorite dish that is served with gravy for main meal or with hot pepper salt as snack.

Ingredients

* 2 pounds fresh perch, butterfish, or trout, cleaned
* 1 teaspoon salt
* juice of ½ lemon
* ½ cup cooking oil
* 1 teaspoon powdered ginger

Directions

1. Season fish with lemon juice, ginger, and salt.
2. Arrange fish on a shallow greased baking tray and brush with oil.
3. Bake in a preheated oven at 300°F until fish is brown and desired crispness is obtained.
4. Cook and serve with hot pepper sauce.

SAMBUSSA (ETHIOPIA)

Samosas are a staple of local cuisine in the Horn of Africa, particularly in Somalia and Ethiopia where they are known as sambussa. While sambusas can be eaten any time of the year, they are usually reserved for special occasions such as Christmas, Meskel, or Ramadan. Due to the long trading history between India and Ethiopia, samosas have been a staple food item for Ethiopians. Samosas are traditionally deep-fried but this recipe has been modified for pan frying.

Ingredients

FILLING

* 1/2 cup yellow onion, thinly sliced
* 1 lb yukon gold potato, peeled and cut into 1/4-inch cubes
* 1/2 cup chopped carrot
* 2 1/2 teaspoons red curry paste
* 1 garlic clove, minced
* 1 cup water
* 1/3 cup light coconut milk
* 2 teaspoons fresh lime juice
* 1/4 teaspoon salt

DOUGH

* 1 teaspoon ground turmeric
* 1/2 teaspoon ground ginger
* 1/2 teaspoon ground cinnamon
* 1 1/2 cups all-purpose flour
* 1/2 teaspoon salt
* 1/4 teaspoon baking soda

* 1/4 cup hot water
* 6 tablespoons fresh lemon juice
7 teaspoons peanut oil, divided

Method

1. To prepare filling, heat a large nonstick skillet over medium-high heat. Coat pan with cooking spray. Add onion and potatoes to pan; sauté 5 minutes or until onion is tender. Reduce heat to low. Add carrot, curry paste, and garlic to pan; cook 5 minutes, stirring occasionally. Add 1 cup water and coconut milk; bring to a simmer. Cook 15 minutes or until liquid almost evaporates and potatoes are tender. Stir in lime juice and 1/4 teaspoon salt. Transfer to a bowl; cool. Partially mash potato mixture with a fork.

2. To prepare dough, combine turmeric, ginger, and cinnamon in a skillet over medium-high heat. Cook 30 seconds or until fragrant, stirring constantly. Transfer to a plate; cool.

3. Lightly spoon flour into dry measuring cups; level with a knife. Place flour, toasted spices, 1/2 teaspoon salt, and baking soda in a food processor; pulse to combine. Combine 1/4 cup hot water, lemon juice, and 1 tablespoon peanut oil in a bowl. Add the hot water mixture through food chute with food processor on, and process until dough forms a ball. Place dough in a bowl coated with cooking spray, turning to coat top. Cover and let rest 15 minutes.

4. Divide dough into 12 equal portions. Working with 1 portion at a time (cover remaining dough to prevent drying), roll on a lightly floured surface to a 4-inch circle. Place 2 tablespoons filling in the center of each dough circle. Moisten edges of dough with water; fold dough over filling to make a half moon. Crimp edges with a fork to seal. Repeat with remaining 11 dough portions and filling to form 12 samosas.

5. Heat 2 teaspoons peanut oil in a large skillet over medium-high heat. Add 6 samosas to pan; cook 3 minutes or until golden brown. Turn and cook 3 minutes or until golden brown. Transfer to a paper towel-lined plate. Repeat procedure with remaining 2 teaspoons peanut oil and remaining 6 samosas. Serve warm with ketchup or cilantro chutney or marmalade as the Ethiopians like.

MATEMEKWANE (BOTSWANA)

Botswana is an African country dominated in geographical term by the Kalahari Desert. Due to the fact that Botswana is an equatorial country the most important dishes are vegetables and fruits. Botswana people eat a lot of stuff with vegetables like soups and salads. They also eat meat that they got from hunting prepared in special tradition with sauces and tomatoes. Favorite meats in Botswana are beef, lamb, goat and chicken. Although bread flour is not part of the staple diet, it has been imported and used in Botswana for a very long time. There are therefore various bread recipes that Botswana can claim as part of its national dishes. The basic ingredients for bread dishes are bread flour, baking powder or yeast, salt, and sometimes sugar. The most common bread dish is matemekwane (dumplings).

Ingredients:

6 cups plain flour
Pinch of salt
2 teaspoons sugar
2 teaspoons instant yeast
1 cup warm water
Oil for frying

Method:

1. Mix all the above ingredients together to make a fairly stiff dough. Knead well for about 2-3 minutes.
2. Cover the dough and let it stand in a warm place until almost doubled in size.
3. Knead and divide into 10-12 balls.
4. Deep fry the dumplings. Serve hot with your favorite dip.

SWORDFISH KEBABS (ANGOLA)

A former colony of Portugal, the Portuguese influence upon Angolan cuisine was subtle but pervasive. The Portuguese brought the European sense of flavoring with spices and techniques of roasting and marinating to the traditional Angolan foods. These influences blended with the local cuisine and produced interesting new recipes. Angolans like their food spicy. Angolan cuisine is varied and tasteful, with local dishes based mainly on fish, cassava products and spicy stews. Swordfish Kebabs are a popular Angolan snack for parties and special occasions.

Ingredients

- o 2 lbs swordfish steaks, cut into large cubes
- o 3 tablespoons olive oil
- o 1/2 lemons, juice of
- o 1 clove garlic, crushed
- o 1 teaspoon paprika
- o 3 tomatoes, quartered
- o 2 small onions, cut into wedges
- o salt & freshly ground black pepper

Directions

1. Place fish in a large dish.
2. Blend together the oil, lemon juice, garlic, paprika and seasonings in a small bowl.
3. Pour over the fish.
4. Cover loosely with clear film and leave in a cool place to marinate for up to 2 hours.
5. Thread the fish cubes onto skewers, alternating with pieces of tomato and onion.
6. Grill the kebabs for 7 to 10 minutes, basting frequently with the remaining marinade and turning occasionally.

CHICKEN STUFFED POTATO PATTIES
(ALGERIA)

Located in North Africa, Algeria is the second largest country on the continent. Its cuisine is eclectic, due to influences from various groups, such as the French, Spanish, Turks and Arabs. Algerian dishes are remarkably flavorful, featuring cumin, caraway, coriander, fennel and other spices. Meals usually include lamb or chicken, and sometimes fish from the Mediterranean. Chicken Stuffed Potato Patties (Makoud Bil Djedj) is a popular snack served in most restaurants, which can also be easily made at home.

Ingredients

* 2 Pounds Potato—peeled
* 2 Medium eggs—beaten
* 1 Medium Onion—finely chopped
* 2 cloves garlic—finely chopped
* 1/4 Teaspoon salt
* 1/4 Teaspoon turmeric
* 1/8 Teaspoon cinnamon
* 6 Sprigs parsley—finely chopped
* 1/2 Pound Chicken Breast—cooked and chopped
* 1/8 Teaspoon cinnamon
* 1/8 Teaspoon pepper
* 1/2 Cup flour—for dusting
* oil—for frying

Directions

1) Cook potatoes in water until soft about 15 minutes. Drain well and mash.
2) Add eggs, Onion, garlic, salt, turmeric, cinnamon and parsley. Mix well.
3) Combine Chicken, cinnamon and pepper. Set aside.
4) Spread flour on cutting board. Put mashed potatoes on the board and flatten into a 3 inch wide by 2 inch deep by 1 foot long log. Make a trench down the center of the log. Put the Chicken into the trench, then pinch the trench shut, covering the Chicken. Cut the log into 8 round patties. Dust with flour.
5) Heat oil in skillet and deep fry until golden brown.
6) Drain and serve. Can be served like a hamburger or just eaten with a side dish.

AKARA (NIGERIA)

Vigna unguiculata (known as black-eyed peas in America; also called black-eyed beans) are native to Asia, the Middle East, and perhaps Africa. They have been grown all over Africa for centuries. In Western Africa they are used to make a batter from which fritters are made. These fritters (known as accra, akara, akla, bean balls,) are commonly prepared at home for breakfast, for snacks, or as an appetizer or side dish. They are also fast-food, sold by vendors on the street, in marketplaces, and at bus stations. Nigerian women carry baskets of Akara on their heads and sell it in streets.

Ingredients

* two to three cups dried black-eyed peas
* one onion, finely chopped
* one-half teaspoon salt
* hot chile pepper, and/or sweet green pepper or sweet red pepper, finely chopped (to taste)
* cayenne pepper or red pepper (to taste)
* one-half teaspoon fresh ginger root, peeled and minced (or a few pinches of powdered ginger) (optional)
* vegetable oil for frying

Method

* Clean the black-eyed peas in running water. Soak them in water for at least a few hours or overnight. After soaking them, rub them together between your hands to remove the skins. Rinse to wash away the skins and any other debris. Drain them in a colander.

* Crush, grind, or mash the black-eyed peas into a thick paste. Add enough water to form a smooth, thick paste of a batter that will cling to a spoon. Add all other ingredients (except oil). Some people allow the batter to stand for a few hours (overnight in the refrigerator); doing so improves the flavor.

* Heat oil in a deep skillet. Beat the batter with a wire whisk or wooden spoon for a few minutes. Make fritters by scooping up a spoon full of batter and using another spoon to quickly push it into the hot oil. Deep fry the fritters until they are golden brown. Turn them frequently while frying. (If the fritters fall apart in the oil, stir in a beaten egg, some cornmeal or crushed breadcrumbs.)

* Serve with an African Hot Sauce or salt, as a snack, an appetizer, or a side dish.

* Variation: Add a half cup of finely chopped leftover cooked meat to the batter before frying; or add a similar amount dried shrimp or prawns.

TAMAYYA (SOUTH AFRICA)

Just as there's more to South Africa than safari, there's a whole lot more to South African food. Here's a mouthwatering overview to one of the most seductive cuisines on earth. South Africa's eclectic cuisine is bursting with competing flavors, hardly surprising given its rich and varied origins. Portuguese, Dutch, French, Moroccan, Indian and even Japanese influences all feature prominently on menus, infused with herbs and spices to give it a unique South African twist. Tamayya (green hamburgers) are healthy vegetable patties packed with fresh greens and dried Beans. The Tamaaya, is stuffed into pockets of bread along with salad, fried Eggplant, potatoes, or just by itself. This sandwich may be eaten for breakfast, lunch or dinner. Bought at the Tamaaya Stand, it is wrapped in paper and eaten as one walks down the street.

Ingredients

* 2 cups broken Beans
* 1/2 cup finely chopped parsley
* 1/4 cup finely chopped coriander
* 1/4 cup finely chopped dill
* 1 cup finely chopped green onions
* 1/2 cup finely chopped Onion (1 small Onion)
* 2 tb finely chopped garlic
* 1 1/2-2 tsp salt, or to taste
* 1/2 tsp pepper, or to taste
* 1 tsp dry coriander powder
* chili powder (optional)
* sesame seeds
* oil for frying

Directions

1. Place the Beans in a large bowl of water and rinse several times until the water is clear. Fill the bowl with at least 6 cups of water, cover and allow them to soak for 2 to 3 days. Wash the greens and dry well, this makes them easier to chop.

2. Remove the tough parts of the stem and then finely chop the leaves and the remaining delicate stems. Measure the greens after they are chopped, but do not pack them down into the cup. Wash the green onions and chop both the white Onion part and the green stem. Chop the Onion and garlic. Drain the Beans and grind very fine.

3. If you are grinding the Beans in a food processor, turn the machine on empty and slowly drop through the tube onto the moving blade. Place the Beans in a bowl and set aside. Add the greens, onions and garlic to the processor, blend well.

4. Add the mashed Beans to the processor and process until the mixture looks green. Transfer the mixture to a bowl, add the spices and baking soda, mix everything until well blended. Cover the bowl and let sit for at least 30 minutes. The longer the better so the flavors blend. If you do not cook all the batter, cover and store in the refrigerator. Heat a medium saute pan, when hot add 1/2 inch of oil and heat until it is hot, lower the heat slightly.

CROQUTTE DE VOLAILLE (MAURITIUS)

Snacks served in Mauritius consist mainly from fresh exotic fruits and vegetables rich in vitamins and proteins. Still besides this natural snacks people of Mauritius like to prepare some special snacks served sometimes also like appetizers or starters. A great Mauritius snack is the one named Croquette de Volaille (Chicken in batter). Allover the country there can be found many Fast food restaurants that offer a great variety of snacks either from the local cuisine or the international one.

Ingredients:

* 125 grams fresh chicken fillet
* 2 teaspoons corn flour
* 1 tablespoon tomato sauce
* Salt & pepper to taste
* Oil (just enough to cover croquettes during frying)

Batter:

* 125 grams self raising flour
* 2 eggs
* 1 teaspoon salt
Water (In small quantities to obtain a thick batter)

Method:

1. Cut chicken into approximately twenty five 1 cm (half inch) pieces.
2. Season the chicken pieces with the tomato sauce, salt and pepper. Set aside to absorb seasoning.
3. Beat up the 2 eggs and 1 tablespoon water.

4. Mix the flour and salt. Gradually blend in the egg mixture. Add water little by little to obtain a thick batter consistency. It should just run off slowly from a tablespoon.

5. Add the corn flour to the chicken pieces and mix thoroughly. Mix the chicken pieces into the batter to uniformly coat every chicken piece.

6. Heat oil (enough to cover croquettes during frying) in a deep frying panto simmering point. Reduce heat to low.

7. Spoon out the chicken pieces one at a time with a batter coating and drop into the simmering oil. Cook to a light golden brown color.

8. Remove cooked croquettes, drain and serve hot with chilli sauce

THE CONTINENT OF ASIA

Geographically, Asia is divided into more natural geographic and cultural sub-regions, including the Central Asia, East Asia, South Asia (the "Indian subcontinent"), North Asia, West Asia and Southeast Asia. In many parts of Asia, rice is a staple food, and it is mostly served steamed or as a porridge known as congee. China is the world largest producer and consumer of rice. An island nation surrounded by ocean, Japan has various fish dishes. Especially, fresh raw fish cuisines are very popular in Japan and around the world, such as Sushi and Sashimi. In India many spices are used in every dish. Most spices originated around India or neighboring countries such as Sri Lanka.

East Asia is usually thought to consist of China, Japan, North Korea, South Korea and Taiwan. The dominant influence historically has been China, though in modern times, cultural exchange has flowed more bi-directionally. Some common vegetables used in Chinese cuisine include Chinese leaves, bok choy (Chinese cabbage), Chinese Spinach (dao-mieu), On Choy, Yu Choy, and gailan (guy-lahn). When it comes to sauces, China is home to soy sauce, which is made from fermented soya beans and wheat. Oyster sauce, transparent rice vinegar, Chinkiang black rice vinegar, fish sauce and fermented tofu (furu) are also widely used. A number of sauces are based on fermented soybeans, including Hoisin sauce, ground bean sauce and yellow bean sauce. Spices and seasonings such as fresh root ginger, garlic, scallion, white pepper, and sesame oil are widely used in many regional cuisines. Sichuan peppercorns, star anise, cinnamon, fennel, and cloves are also used. To provide extra flavors to dishes, many Chinese cuisines also contain dried Chinese mushrooms, dried baby shrimps, dried tangerine peel, and dried Sichuan chillies as well. In most dishes in Chinese cuisine, food is prepared in bite-sized pieces, ready for direct picking up and eating.

South Asia (Indian Subcontinent): Just as Japanese sushi relies on the freshness of the meat and Chinese food relies on the various sauces to impart the right flavor and taste, Indian food relies on the spices in which it is cooked. Spices have always been considered to be India's prime commodity. It is interesting to see an Indian cook at work, with a palette of spices, gratuitously sprinkling these powders in exact pinches into the dish in front of him/her. Most of the Indian food available abroad, is the North Indian and Pakistani type that include meat and chicken dishes, Indian cottage cheese called paneer, pilaus garnished with fried onions and roasted nuts like cashew. 'Tandoori' food, a favorite with many foreigners is a gift from the Punjab. Various meats are marinated with spices, ginger and garlic pastes and curd and roasted over a primitive clay-pot(tandoor) with a wood-fire burning underneath. The special wheat bread cooked over the tandoor is called 'Naan'.

Southeast Asia is usually thought to include Burma, Thailand, Laos, Cambodia, Vietnam, Malaysia, Singapore, Brunei, Indonesia, the Philippines and East Timor. The rich culture of South East Asia lies at the tastiest food in the world. Once known as the land of the spices, the food of the Thais, Filipinos, Vietnamese, and Indonesians are among the most famous exotic creations. Much of the identity of South East Asia lies on the different food that come from unique, yet common backgrounds following the influences of Indian, Chinese, and the European colonizers along with the local flavor. The food has both common and binding ingredients. These include coconut milk, lemon grass, sugar, basil, fish paste, and chili. To an outsider's taste buds, this food is described as spicy, tangy and sweet, all mixing together to present a unique taste. Curry, which is an Indian food, has evolved to be a staple dish in South East Asia. Thai food is the most popular cuisine coming from South East Asia. It takes in five different flavors from the different regions in its traditional kingdoms which are sour, salty, sweet, spicy, and bitter. The famous southern curries are traditional Indian adaptations that have local ingredients like coconut milk. Thai food uses generous servings of fresh spices and fish sauces. Like any other Asian country, rice is the staple food of the Thais. The most famous dishes are Pad Thai, and Red Na.

West Asia largely corresponds with the term the Middle East. West Asia consists of Turkey, Syria, Armenia, Georgia, Azerbaijan, Iraq, Iran, Lebanon, Jordan, Israel, Palestinian territories, Saudi Arabia, Kuwait, Bahrain, Qatar, United Arab Emirates, Oman and Yemen. Central Asia is deemed to consist of the five former Soviet Socialist Republics: Kazakhstan,

Kyrgyzstan, Tajikstan, Uzbekistan and Turkmenistan. However, Iran, Afghanistan and Pakistan are sometimes included. Cuisine of these areas is one of the most prominent cuisines of Asia, with cuisines from Pakistan, India, China and Azerbaijan especially showing significant influence. One of the most famous Central Asian foods are manti and pilaf.

SAMOSAS (INDIA)

To start the Super Snacks series of the Asian continent, what better snack could there be than the world famous Samosas from India—the deep-fried stuffed patties (meat/vegetable)

Meat Stuffing

2lbs ground lamb or chicken
2 medium sized yellow onions (finely minced)
6 pods of garlic (minced)
2 large tomatoes (finely chopped)
1 green chili (minced)
2 teaspoons salt
1 teaspoon red chili powder
1 teaspoon black pepper powder
1 teaspoon cumin seeds
2 teaspoons coriander powder
2 green cardamoms
6 tablespoons oil

Heat the oil in heavy-based saucepan on medium heat. Add minced onions, cumin seeds, black pepper and cardamoms. Stir-fry for 10 minutes or till onions are golden brown. Add meat and stir-fry for 10 minutes. Add garlic, green chili and tomatoes. Stir-fry for 10 minutes. Cover the pan and let meat simmer on low heat for 20 minutes. Remove the lid and cook for a few more minutes till all liquid is dried up. Set aside for cooling.

Vegetable Stuffing

2lbs boiled potatoes (mashed)
1 cup green peas
2 green chilies (chopped)
1 large onion (chopped)
2 teaspoons salt
1 teaspoon black pepper (freshly ground)
1 teaspoon red chili powder
2 tablespoons finely chopped cilantro
4 tablespoons oil

Stir-fry all the ingredients for 5 minutes.

Ingredients for Dough

3 cups all purpose flour
3 tablespoons oil
½ teaspoon salt
1-1/2 cup water

Make firm dough (kneading for about 5 minutes). Divide the dough into 30 small balls. Roll each ball into 4-inch round. Cut each roll to half. Make a coned shaped triangle of each half roll and fill it with the cooked meat/vegetable stuffing. Seal the triangle's open side pressing with moistened fingers. Heat oil in a wok or large frying pan to 300 degrees. Deep-fry Samosas till golden brown.

Serve with mint and cilantro chutney/tomato ketchup.

CHICKEN TIKKA (INDIA)

This snack's stunning popularity has spread far beyond India's borders to make it U.K. and Europe's most ordered snack on any menu. The word Tikka means bits, pieces or chunks. Chicken Tikka is an easy-to-cook dish in which chicken chunks are marinated in special spices and then grilled on skewers. Chicken Tikka can also be made into Chicken Tikka Masala, a tasty gravy dish.

Ingredients:

* 1 cup fresh yoghurt (should not be sour)
* 1 cup finely chopped fresh coriander leaves
* 2 tbsps ginger paste
* 3 tbsps garlic paste
* 3-4 tbsps garam masala
* 6 peppercorns/ 2 dry red chillies
* 3 tbsps lime/ lemon juice
* 1/2 tsp orange food coloring
* 1 kg chicken (breast or thigh) skinless and cut into 2" chunks
* 1 large onion cut into very thin rings
* Lime/ Lemon wedges to garnish
* 1 tsp Chaat Masala (available at most Indian groceries)

Preparation:

* Grind the chopped coriander (keep some aside for garnishing) and all other marinade ingredients (except yoghurt) to a smooth paste in a food processor.

* Pour the above mix into a large bowl and add yoghurt. Mix well. Add the chicken pieces and mix well. Cover the bowl and refrigerate. Allow to marinate overnight.

* Thread the chicken onto skewers and keep ready.

* Preheat your oven or grill to a medium high temperature (200 C/ 400F/ Gas Mark 6).

* Place the skewers on the grill racks in your oven with a tray underneath to catch drippings. Roast open till the chicken is browned on all sides and tender.

* Remove from skewers and put the chicken in a plate.

* Put the onion rings in a separate bowl and squeeze lime juice over them. Now sprinkle the chaat masala over them and mix well so the onions are fully coated.

* Garnish the Chicken Tikka with these onion rings and serve.

TALI MACHCHI (PAKISTAN)

Tali Machchi (fried fish) is one of the most popular snacks in Pakistan. It is a popular street snack which is available in plenty with the street corner venders in Pakistan. The snack is also popular in India as an evening snack, more popularly known as fish-pakoras.

Ingredients

1-1/2 lb fish steaks
2 cloves garlic
1-1/2 teaspoon salt
1 teaspoon freshly grated ginger
½ teaspoon ground turmeric
½ teaspoon ground black pepper
¼ teaspoon chili powder
Lemon juice
Oil for frying
Fresh coriander leaves to garnish
Lemon wedges to garnish

Method

Wash fish and dry on paper towels

Crush garlic with salt, mix with ginger, turmeric, pepper, chili powder and enough lemon juice to make a paste. Rub the paste well over the fish on both sides, cover and leave fot 20 minutes.

In a large frying pan heat just enough oil to cover base of pan and when hot, put in the fish steaks. Fry on medium heat until cooked, then turn slices carefully and fry other side.

Serve on platter garnished with coriander lesves and lemon wedges.

KEBAB ROLLS (AFGHANISTAN)

There are not many Afghani snacks in the cuisine of Afghanistan. Some of them are traditional, whereas the others have been greatly influenced by other continental cuisines. The Afghani snacks usually contain nuts, dried fruits, pistachio and traditional sweetened milk and Khati cookies. One of the most popular Afghani snacks is Kebab rolls. These are made out of lamb or chicken meat rolled in the traditional nann (whole-wheat flat bread) which is served with home made spicy chutneys, pickles etc. They're prepped and marinated a day ahead, and then grilled before guests even cross the doorstep, freeing you up to enjoy the party without fretting that something's burning in the kitchen.

Ingredients

4 large cloves garlic, minced
¾ cup plain yogurt
1 tsp. ground cumin
1 ½ tsp. ground turmeric
2 tbsp. lemon juice
1 tsp. Kosher salt
1 tsp. black pepper
2 lbs. boneless lamb, cut into 3/4-inch cubes
Small wooden or metal skewers
Ground sumac (optional)
Cilantro Mint Chutney

Method

In a medium bowl mix together the garlic, yogurt, spices, lemon juice, salt and pepper. Add the lamb and mix well. Cover and refrigerate at least 4 hours, preferably overnight.

An hour before you are ready to cook, pull the lamb from the refrigerator. If you are using wooden skewers immerse them in water for 20 minutes.

Spear 3 to 4 pieces of lamb on each skewer and set aside until you are ready to cook. Grill the kebabs over a medium-high flame until cooked through but still pink in the center. If you don't have a grill, cook the kebabs under a broiler in your oven.

Coat the bottom of your serving platter with a few tablespoons of chutney. Set the kebabs on top of the chutney with a little crock of the remaining chutney in the center.

BARA (NEPAL)

Nepali food, especially ethnic Newari food is rich in varieties of appetizers, snacks or hors d'oeuvres. Many of these appetizers may be fried and may not be comparatively lower in fat than western appetizers heavy on butter. Bara (Black Lentil Deep Fried Patties) is one of the favorite Nepali appetizers.

Ingredients

1 cup black lentil
1 table spoon ginger paste or ginger juice
1/4 tea spoon asafetida (Hing)
1/2 tea spoon Cumin Powder (Jeera)
Oil enough to deep fry
Salt to taste

Preparation

1   Soak black lentil in water overnight or until the black coating is easily removed.
2   Remove black coating by rinsing with water.
3   Grind into a paste with minimum water.
4   Add all the spices to the lentil and mix well.
5   Heat the oil for deep fry.
6   Make a patty shape out of lentil in a plate. Make a hole in the patty like that in donut.
7   Carefully put it in the hot oil and cook golden brown in both sides.
8   Serve hot or cold.

POTENT POTATOES (BHUTAN)

Every region which is a part of the country of Bhutan has its own specialty, as a result of different influences. Although meat is considered very delicious and consistent in the Bhutanese cuisine, the slaughter of animals is forbidden here and this is because Bhutan is a Buddhist country. In any case, this does not represent a problem, as people can replace meat with any kind of vegetarian dish consisting of cheese and chili. Potent Potatoes is one such dish which is considered a delicacy.

Ingredients

1. 4 large baking potatoes
2. 1/4-1/2 cup oil or clarified butter
3. 2-3 chopped onions
4. 1/4-1/2 cup ginger-root, finely minced
5. 1-2 tablespoon minced garlic
6. 1 teaspoon black pepper
7. 1/2 teaspoon turmeric
8. 1/4 teaspoon Cayenne or crushed red pepper flakes
9. 8 whole cloves
10. 1/2 teaspoon ground cardamom
11. 1/2 teaspoon ground cinnamon
13. Salt (to taste)
14. 1/2 pint cottage cheese (optional)

Directions

Scrub potatoes, rub with small amount of oil, and bake at 400° until well done. Heat clarified butter or oil in large skillet. Saute onions and ginger until they begin to brown and then add garlic and spices and cook for 4-5 minutes longer. Add a little water if necessary. Add salt. Stir and remove from heat. Cut baked potatoes in half lengthwise. Scoop out insides, and combine with Onion mixture. Add cottage cheese. Broil until Cheese is melted and bubbly. Serve hot.

BISCUTLUS (MALDIVES)

Maldives islands are located in the Indian Ocean which surrounds the islands. Indian Ocean provides Maldives inhabitants with their main source of protein, with fish, while vegetables are used as fillings. Asian elements are obvious by the great use of spices such as curry or some Asian hot sauces. People from Maldives serve fish, generally Tuna, for almost every meal of the day. Fish combined with onions, chilies, lemon juice, coconut and rice structures the essential diet. Biscutlus (Tuna cutlets) is a popular snack of Maldives.

Ingredients

2 tins Tuna
250 g Potato (mashed)
2 Onions (sliced thinly)
1 Garlic Clove (crushed)
2 Cherry Pepper (sliced thinly)
Juice of 2 Limes
1 tsp Peppercorns (ground)
6 Eggs (hard boiled and cut into halves)
200 g bread-crumbs
2 Eggs
Salt to season
Oil for deep-frying

Method

Crush the onion, garlic and chilli with salt. Add in the lime and mix in well. Add in the mashed potato, tuna and pepper.

Combine the ingredients thoroughly. Divide the mixture to 12 equal sized balls. Stick half of each egg with the tuna and potato mixture and form an oval shape. Pané the prepared cutlets, deep fry until golden brown. Drain on absorbent kitchen paper. Serve hot.

BOOTHEE JAW (MYANMAR)

Burmese people adore fried snacks (a-jaw zohn) at any time of the day, whether at a pavement stall with a sour chilli dip on the side and a cup of green tea or at home as a side dish in a main meal. Gourd fritters (boothee jaw), tofu fritters (topu jaw) and bean fritters (baya jaw) are the two best-known snacks that originate in Myanmar. It is a tradition to offer these snacks to visitors who come to a Burmese house. Crispy gourd or onion fritters are essential garnishes for Traditional fish noodle soup. These dishes, as most of the Burmese dishes, are served on the floor, at a lower table.

Ingredients

4 tablespoons ground rice flour
4 tablespoons self-raising flour
1 tablespoon sticky/glutinous rice flour
1 tablespoon chickpea flour
¼ teaspoon baking powder
½ teaspoon salt
1 tablespoon oil
75ml ice cold water
Oil for deep frying
200g bitter gourd, sliced into 1cm thick strips

Method

Put all the dry ingredients in a mixing bowl and add the oil. Stirring continuously, add the cold water a little at a time until incorporated. Leave the batter in the fridge to rest for 30 minutes. Meanwhile prepare the vegetables for frying.

A deep-fat fryer is ideal but if you don't have one, heat the oil in a medium-sized saucepan (never fill the pan more than halfway). When the oil is hot, dip the gourd in the batter just before you drop it into the oil.

Deep fry in batches for 5-10 minutes or until golden brown, turning occasionally. Drain on kitchen paper and serve while still warm.

MASALA VADEI (SRI LANKA)

Vada or vadei (as called in Sri Lanka), is a doughnut shaped South Indian snack made from lentils or potatoes. Another type of vada commonly known Aama Vadai is made entirely of lentils. Vada is eaten throughout South India in many forms along with sambar, coconut chutney or rassam. Vada is popular in many forms all over India. Dahi vada, batata vada, paruppu vada, thairu vada, masala vada, rava vada and ulli vada being some of the most popular ones. In Sri Lanka Masala Vadei is a very popular snack.

Ingredients:

Bengalgram dhall 1 cup
(Split pea) ginger 1' piece cummin seeds 1 tbs onion 2 green chillies
4 salt
Curry leaves
Coriander leaves oil for frying

Method:

Soak bengalgram dhall for 2-3 hours. Then grind it with ginger coarsly. to this add chopped onion, chopped green chillies, cumin seeds Chopped curry & coriander leaves and salt. Mix well. Make small patties. Deep fry it.

PUCHKA (BANGLADESH)

Bangladesh was eastern part of Bengal before partition, hence the two regions share similarities in cuisine. However, it also has considerable regional variations. A staple across the country is rice, various kinds of lentil and fish, which features as the major source of protein in the Bangladeshi diet.

Bangladeshi food is spicy. The most important spices in Bangladeshi cuisine are garlic, ginger, coriander, cumin, turmeric and chilli. Puchka is an enormously popular spicy snack. This is the lip-smacking Bengali version of the ubiquitous paani puri.

Ingredients:

To make puri:

> 1 cup Semolina (Rava / Suji)
> 3 tblsp Fine Wheat Flour (Maida)
> 1/4 tsp Baking Soda
> Oil to deep fry

To make pani:

> 1/2 cup Tamarind (Imli) Pulp
> 2 cups Water
> 2 tblsp roasted Cumin Seed (Jeera) Powder
> 2 tblsp un-roasted Cumin Seed (Jeera)
> Coriander Leaves
> 3 Green Chilly (Hari Mirch)
> 2 tblsp Mint Leaves (Pudina Leaves) Chutney
> 1 tblsp Black Salt (kala namak)
> 2 tblsp Jaggary (Gur)

How to make pani puri:

* To make pani:

* Measure all ingredients.

* Adjust spices and tangyness to taste.

* Strain through a wire strainer to remove any rough bits.

* To make puri:

* Mix sooji, maida, baking soda, salt and enough water to knead a soft dough.

* Stand covered with wet cloth for 15-20 minutes.

* Make small sized balls.

* With the help of some dry maida or sooji, roll into thin rounds.

* Heat oil in a pan and deep fry puris till very light brown and crisp.

* Drain in a paper towel for a while to dry out the oil.

* Store in an airtight container when cool.

KUIH KODOK (MALAYSIA)

Malaysian cuisine is yummy, exotic and exciting. Comprising of three main groups namely Malay, Chinese and Indian, Malaysian food has become a fusion of the three and more, making it one of the world's most unique cuisine. One of the most popular Malaysian snacks in the Malaysian cuisine are the Dim sum which are steamed snacks that can be found at hotel outlets, large chain restaurants. Dim sum is like the Chinese version of the Japanese sushi. The difference is this: dim sum is hot while sushi is cold. Another famous Malaysian snack is Kuih Kodok. This is basically Malaysian-style fried banana snack—bananas all mashed up with flour, eggs, sugar, and then deep fried.

Ingredients:

3 big ripe bananas
1 1/2 cup flour
1 1/2 tablespoon sugar
1 egg
Some water
Oil for deep frying

Method:

Break the bananas (with hands) into small pieces and put them into a bowl. Add flour, egg, sugar, and some water. Use a big spoon and stir the ingredients so they are well blended.

Heat up a frying pan and add some cooking oil for deep frying. Once the oil is heated, scoop up a spoonful of batter into the frying pan. Try to "shape" the batter so it's somewhat round. Deep fry until golden brown.

THAI GOLDEN CUPS (THAILAND)

The uniqueness of Thai taste has charmed and impressed all lovers of gourmet cuisine across the world. Krathong Thong, which means golden cups in Thai, is one of the foremost menus that come to mind when think of Thai food. A popular Thai appetizer. it is a light dish, yet one that teases you to want more. The golden pastry cups filled with minced chicken and chopped vegetables are cute little cups that are very attractive and impressive. These light crispy golden cups can be filled with various savory fillings, including shredded pork and prawns mixed with sliced young corn, coriander root, garlic, pepper and fish sauce. The cups are filled just before serving and garnished with red chillies flakes and cilantro leaves, to retain crispiness of the pastry.

Ingredients

Patty Cups

½ cup rice flour
6 tablespoons white flour
4 tablespoons thin coconut milk
2 tablespoons tapioca starch
1 egg yolk
¼ teaspoon sugar
¼ teaspoon salt
¼ teaspoon soda oil for deep-frying

Filling

2 tablespoons oil
4 tablespoons finely diced onion
2 cups finely chopped cooked chicken

¼ cup corn kernels
2 tablespoons finely diced carrot
1 tablespoon sugar
¼ teaspoon black soy sauce
½ teaspoon salt
½ teaspoon ground white pepper
Cilantro leaves for garnish
1 red chili, finely sliced

Method

To prepare the cups, a special brass mold with a long handle is used. To make the patty cups, mix all ingredients except oil together in a bowl. Heat oil. Dip the mold in the oil to heat. Dip the hot mold in the batter and plunge back into oil. The thin shell that forms around the mold is fried for about 5 minutes until light brown, to create pleated golden cup. Then shake to remove the cup from the mold. Drain on paper towels. Repeat until batter is all used up.

To make the filling, put the oil in a hot wok and stir-fry onion and chicken for 2 minutes. Add the rest of the ingredients and fry for 3 minutes until the vegetables are fairly soft. Let it cool.

Divide the filling between the cups. Garnish with cilantro and red chili flakes.

Try the recipe and enjoy.

CURRY PUFFS (SINGAPORE/MALAYSIA)

Curry puff is a Malaysian, Singaporean and Thai snack which is of Malay origin. Curry puffs look like crispy dumplings or large samosas. Because Singapore is so diverse culturally, no one knows exactly where the dish came from originally, and some even say it came from the U.K. No matter where it came from, curry puffs are the most popular afternoon snack in Singapore. It is a small pie consisting of specialized curry with chicken and potatoes in a deep-fried or baked pastry shell. The curry is quite thick to prevent it from oozing out of the snack. A common snack in the region, the curry puff is one of several "puff"-type pastries with different fillings, though now it is by far the most common. Other common varieties include sardines and onions or sweet fillings such as yam. In Indian food stalls in Malaysia, it is quite common to find vegetarian curry puffs with potatoes, carrots and onions as fillings. The Malay curry puffs tend to be sweet while the Indian curry puffs are usually spicy.

Ingredients

Filling

5 tablespoons oil
1 medium red or yellow onion, finely chopped
1 teaspoon curry powder
1 teaspoon cayenne or red chili powder
½ teaspoon turmeric powder
2 cups finely diced cooked chicken
2 large potatoes, boiled and finely diced
1-1/2 teaspoon sugar
½ teaspoon black pepper salt to taste

Pastry

4 cups white flour
10 tablespoons butter or margarine
14 tablespoons water salt to taste oil for deep frying

Method

To make the filling, heat oil and fry onion gently until golden brown. Add the curry powder, cayenne and turmeric and fry gently. Add the chicken, potatoes, sugar, pepper and salt and cook for 5 minutes. Mix well and leave aside to cool.

To make the pastry, mix flour with butter or margarine, water and salt and knead well. Let it rest for 30 minutes. Divide the dough into small balls and roll into 3 inches diameter rounds. Take a tablespoon of filling and place in center. Fold pastry over to make a half circle and crimp the edges. Heat oil in wok and deep fry until golden brown. Serve hot with cilantro chutney.

TEMPURA (JAPAN)

One of the triumphs of Japanese cooking—a fried food that is light and fresh-tasting rather than heavy and greasy, Tempura is a popular Japanese dish of deep-fried battered meats, seafood or vegetables. It's a cooking style in which the essence of the ingredient itself completely defines the taste. In Japan, restaurants specializing in tempura are called tempura-ya and range from inexpensive fast food chains to very expensive five-star restaurants. Many restaurants offer tempura as part of a set meal or an obento (lunch box), and it is also a popular ingredient in take-out or convenience store obento boxes. Outside Japan (as well as recently in Japan), restaurants sometimes use broccoli, zucchini and asparagus. American restaurants are known to serve tempura in the form of various meats, particularly chicken, and cheeses, usually mozzarella.

Ingredients (vegetable/shrimp tempura)

    1 onion
    8 cauliflower florets
    16 green beans
    8 mushroom heads
    1 potato
    8 shrimp (medium)

Batter

    2 cups all purpose flour
    2 eggs (yolk)
    1 cup tap water

Dip

6-inch white radish
2 tablespoons Japanese soy sauce
2 tablespoons lemon juice
2 tablespoons chicken stock
1 tablespoon sugar

Method

First make the dip. Heat soy sauce with sugar and stock. Add pinch of salt and pepper. Let it cool in a bowl. Add lemon juice and pour on grated radish. Dip is ready.

Peal and cut onion in 1/4inch slices. Secure the onion slices with toothpicks. Cut sweet potatoes into 1/8-inch slices and dip them in cold water. Wash mushroom heads, dry them with paper towel. Cut the ends of green beans. Peel the shrimp but keep the tails. Pat dry them and take out any liquid left in them.

Prepare the batter. Beat the egg yolk in a large bowl. Add cold water and beat to mix. Add flour and mix thoroughly. Batter is ready.

Dip vegetables/shrimp in batter and deep fry in small batches on medium heat. Serve hot with the dip.

SPRING ROLLS (CHINA)

Shuen Guen, popularly known world over as Spring Rolls, is a traditional Chinese snack, made with a round, thin dough sheet with fillings rolled inside and deep fried in oil. Spring rolls are usually eaten during the Spring Festival in China, hence the name. It is a very popular snack in several Asian countries, most notably China, Vietnam, the Philippines and Indonesia. The snacks are crisp outside and fresh inside, really delicious. Spring rolls vary slightly from place to place, with well-known types being Shanghai Spring Rolls and Fuzhou Spring Rolls.

Ingredients

20 medium frozen spring roll wrappers, 9in square, defrosted
1 egg white lightly beaten
2 cups vegetable oil for deep-frying

For the filling:

3 tablespoons vegetable oil
1lb carrots cut into thin strips
1/4lb cabbage, finely shredded
7oz canned sliced bamboo shoots, rinsed and cut into thin strips
3/4lb snow peas or thin green beans, thinly sliced on the diagonal
8 shitake mushrooms, stems removed and cups thinly sliced
2 teaspoons finely chopped fresh ginger
3 teaspoons light soy sauce
6oz noodles, soaked in hot water for 5 minutes and cut into short lengths
8 scallions cut into rounds salt and freshly ground black pepper to taste

Method

For the filling, heat the oil in a wok. Add the carrots, cabbage and bamboo shoots and stir-fry for 2 minutes. Add the snow peas or green beans, mushrooms, the ginger and soy sauce and stir-fry for 3 minutes. Add the noodles and scallions and stir-fry rapidly for 2 minutes, until the liquid evaporates but the vegetables are still moist. Season to taste, remove from the wok and let cool.

Place one spring roll wrapper on a flat surface. Put about 2 tablespoons of the cold filling on the corner nearest to you. Flatten the filling a little, then roll the corner of the wrapper over it, toward the center. Fold in the two side flaps. Brush the far corner of the wrapper with a little of the egg white and continue rolling to make a well-sealed bundle. Repeat with the remaining filling and wrappers.

Heat the oil in a deep-fat frier or wok. Add 4 spring rolls, lower the heat a little, and deep fry for 6-8 minutes, turning the rolls several times until golden brown. Remove from the wok with a slotted spoon and drain on paper towels. Keep the spring rolls hot in a warm oven until the remaining batches are fried, then serve immediately. Alternately, leave the cooked rolls until cold, then briefly refry just before serving.

The cooked spring rolls can be frozen for up to 4 weeks. To serve, heat the oil and deep fry the frozen rolls for 6-8 minutes.

PASTEIS DE NATA (MACAU)

Pastéis de Nata (egg tarts), these are a Portuguese-style egg tart that actually originated from Coloane here in Macau. The delicious custard tart has become a featured snack of the city, just like the Roast Duck of Beijing. Margaret's Café & Nata and Lord Stow's Café, to be found on the Macau Peninsular and Taipa Island respectively are the two best places to buy these tarts. Tourists often buy some as gifts for friends and families.

Ingredients

* 1 cup milk
* 3 tablespoons cornstarch
* 1/2 vanilla bean
* 1 cup white sugar
* 6 egg yolks
* 1 (17.5 ounce) package frozen puff pastry, thawed

Directions

1. Preheat oven to 375 degrees F (190 degrees C.) Lightly grease 12 muffin cups and line bottom and sides with puff pastry.
2. In a saucepan, combine milk, cornstarch, sugar and vanilla. Cook, stirring constantly, until mixture thickens. Place egg yolks in a medium bowl. Slowly whisk 1/2 cup of hot milk mixture into egg yolks. Gradually add egg yolk mixture back to remaining milk mixture, whisking constantly. Cook, stirring constantly, for 5 minutes, or until thickened. Remove vanilla bean.
3. Fill pastry-lined muffin cups with mixture and bake in preheated oven for 20 minutes, or until crust is golden brown and filling is lightly browned on top

CHICKEN-KIEV (MONGOLIA)

The Mongolians have only a few recipes of snacks. Their main meals feature very consistent food, but there is sometimes a need for foods that are served only between the major tables. Some of the Mongolian snacks, such as Chicken-Kiev, is inspired by the cuisine of other nations. Most of the Mongolian snacks are based on meats. A few examples are: Deboned Chicken Morsels, Mongolian Beef Sandwiches and Red-Cooked Mongolian Lamb.

Ingredients

1. 2 lbs boneless skinless Chicken breasts (6 Chicken halves)
2. 1 cup butter, at room temperature
3. 1/2 teaspoon black pepper
4. 1 teaspoon granulated garlic powder
5. 2 large eggs
6. 3 tablespoons cold water
7. 1/4 teaspoon black pepper
8. 1/4 teaspoon granulated garlic powder
9. 3/4 teaspoon dried dill weed
10. 1/2 cup all-purpose flour
11. 3/4 cup fine dry breadcrumbs or saltine crumbs
12. 1/2 medium lemon, sliced
13. 1/4 cup finely chopped fresh parsley
14. 2 cups vegetable oil or extra virgin olive oil

Directions

1. Remove all fat from Chicken and discard.
2. If Chicken breasts are in one piece, split them into two pieces.

3. Place each Chicken breast between two pieces of wax paper and using a mallet, pound Chicken until about 1/8 inch thickness.

4. DO NOT POUND TOO HARD THAT THE Chicken BREAKS UP.

5. Place on a dish, cover and set prepared Chicken breasts aside.

6. In a small mixing bowl, mix together butter, black pepper, granulated garlic powder and mix to combine well.

7. Form butter into a 2" x 3" rectangular shape on a 6 inch square piece of aluminum foil; thickness should be about 1/4".

8. Place in freezer compartment of refrigerator for about 1/2 hour until butter mixture hardens.

9. Cut butter into 6 equal pieces (1/2" x 3").

10. Place one piece of butter at the front of each prepared Chicken breast.

11. Fold in edges just to catch the edges of the butter on each side, then roll the chciken breast to encase the butter completely.

12. This is necessary so that the butter does not run out while deep-frying.

13. Secure Chicken rolls with skewers or toothpicks.

14. In a bowl, beat eggs with water.

15. In a separate mixing bowl, mix together black pepper, garlic powder, dill weed and flour.

16. In another separate bowl, measure the bread crumbs.

17. Completely coat each rolled Chicken into the flour mixture.

18. Dip flour coated Chicken into the egg mixture.

19. Now roll and coat the Chicken in the bread crumbs.

20. Place Chicken in a shallow dish and chill for about 30 minutes.

21. In a medium size frying pan, add vegetable oil and heat to medium-high heat.

22. Carefully place the Chicken rolls into the oil and cook for 5 minutes on each side or until Chicken is done and golden brown.

23. To test for doneness, cut into 1 rolled Chicken to make sure no pink is showing.

24. Serve immediately, garnished with lemon twists and parsley.

FISH BALLS (HONG KONG)

Snacking is a way of life for Hong Kong people, and females are the biggest 'snackers' in spite of always claiming to be watching their weight. According to various studies, there were more than 300 kiosks selling street snacks throughout Hong Kong—and growing. While Hong Kong people don't need a reason to snack, the Chinese New Year is just an occasion where they will buy them in abundance for themselves and friends. Among all street snack items, the most favorite snack is Fish Balls among Hong Kong people.

Ingredients

1/2 pound flaked fish
1/3 cup saltine cracker crumbs
1 large egg, beaten
2 teaspoons finely minced green onion tops or leeks
1 tablespoon mayonnaise
1 teaspoon Worcestershire sauce
1 teaspoon grain mustard
1/4 teaspoon hot red pepper sauce
Bread crumbs
Oil for frying
Parsley, lemon wedges for garnish
Dipping sauce if desired

Method

Any type of fish you prefer will be fine for this recipe. If using raw fish, grind or chop meat really fine. If already cooked, just flake it into a bowl. Stir in the next seven ingredients and roll into bite size balls. Place on parchment or wax paper and refrigerate several hours to firm.

Roll each ball into bread crumbs to coat returning them to the paper. Heat a half inch of oil in a frying pan (or use a deep fryer for faster results) and heat until almost smoking. Add a few balls at a time frying on all sides until golden brown. Remove to paper towels to drain and cook remaining balls. Keep warm until ready to serve by placing in a low heated oven or warming tray.

Arrange on serving tray garnished with the parsley and lemon slices if desired. Serve with your favorite dipping sauce.

MURTABAK (BRUNEI)

State of Brunei is a country located on the north coast of the island of Borneo, in Southeast Asia. Apart from its coastline with the South China Sea it is completely surrounded by the state of Sarawak, Malaysia. The Sultanate of Brunei at one time was ranked as the richest man in the world. The cuisine of Brunei has been greatly influenced by neighboring Malaysia and Singapore, as well as the many ethnic Chinese living there. Local food is similar to Malay cuisine with fresh fish and rice, often quite spicy. Hawker-style Food is always a favorite throughout Southeast Asia. Murtabak (Meat Crepes) is a popular snack.

Ingredients

* Clarified Butter (or substitute with cooking oil)
* 4 Eggs
* 1 lb plain flour
* 3/4 teaspoon fine salt
* 1/2 teaspoon pepper
* 1/4 teaspoon baking powder

Meat Filling

* 20 oz minced mutton
* 1/2 teaspoon salt
* 1/4 teaspoon salt
* 1/4 teaspoon turmeric powder
* 20 oz onions (diced)
* 20 cardamoms, seeded
* 2 heaped tablespoons roasted coriander seeds
* 1 level tablespoon aniseed

Directions

Meat Filling

1. Fry turmeric in a little oil. Set aside for later. Cook mutton with rest of ingredients and add turmeric. season to taste.

Dough

1. Mix flour and baking powder together into a bowl with 12 fl oz of water. Knead into a smooth dough. Cover bowl and leave dough overnight.
2. Divide dough into 4 equal portions. Roll out thinly on an oiled marble top (or glass cutting board). Spread liberally with butter/oil. Fold and shape into balls. Cover dough with a damp cloth. Set aside for 1/2 hour.
3. Roll out each dough piece into a thin rectangle. Place filling evenly in centre of dough. Pat lightly beaten egg over meat. Wrap dough over meat to form a square. Fry in hot butter/oil till brown on both sides. Serve hot.

KHMER SHRIMP PATTIES (CAMBODIA)

Shrimp is a very common Cambodian ingredient, together with other sea food delicacies. Num Pa Kon Chien (Khmer shrimp patties) is a very popular snack along with other dishes such as the Turmeric Fried Fish, Cambodian Fishcakes, Steamed Trout with Spring Onions.

Ingredients

  * 1 lb ground shrimp
  * 1 clove garlic
  * 2 chopped green onions
  * 1/4 tsp soy sauce
  * 1/2 tsp fish sauce
  * 1/4 tsp sugar
  * 1 tsp paprika
  * 1/4 tsp black pepper
  * 1 egg (white only)
  * 1 cup flour
  * Oil for frying

Method

In a large bowl, mix ground shrimp, garlic, onions, soy sauce, fish sauce, sugar, paprika and black pepper. Mix well.

Add the egg-white and the flour. Mix well, forming into small patties. Use a little flour to better handle the patties. Set aside.

Heat a frying pan to medium heat. Add oil. Pan fry shrimp patties in peanut oil until both sides are golden.

KAIPEN (LAOS)

Kaipen is a fresh water moss, sort of a Laotian "seaweed" similiar to Japanese Nori. It is extremely rich in iron and is an excellent source of fiber. It is a very popular street snack in Laos and Thailand. Kaipen is available at Whole Foods stores and Asian Markets.

Ingredients

1/2 cup vegetable oil
1/4 cup finely chopped ginger
1/2 cup garlic, peeled and sliced, about 1/2 head
1/4 cup sugar
2 tablespoons dried chile flakes, or to taste
1/4 cup Thai or Vietnamese fish sauce
1 sheet kaipen, cut in rectangles 2 by 4 inches.

Method

1. Heat 2 tablespoons oil in skillet. Add ginger, and sauté over low heat until it starts to turn translucent. Add garlic, and stir until golden. Drain well, and spoon ginger and garlic from skillet to mortar. Pound to a paste.
2. Pour off all but thin film of oil from skillet. Add sugar, chili and fish sauce. Cook over very low heat about 5 minutes, stirring constantly, until sugar dissolves and sauce becomes syrupy. Stir in ginger and garlic and cook a minute or so longer to form thick sauce. Check seasoning; add more chili or fish sauce if needed, so that dip is quite spicy with a salty tang. Set aside to cool to room temperature.
3. In clean skillet, heat remaining oil to very hot. Fry kaipen briefly, turning once, until crisp. Fold and place on paper towels to drain. Cool to room temperature, and serve with a dip.

PA JUN (KOREA)

This Korean scallion pancake recipe is easy to make and is always a big crowd-pleaser. It works as a hearty snack, an appetizer, or a side dish to a Korean or Asian meal. As with most Korean recipes and dishes, you can tweak it to your own tastes. Carrots, zucchini, mushrooms, and kimchi are also popular fillings for Korean scallion pancakes.

Ingredients:

* 2 cups flour
* 2 eggs, beaten
* 1.5 cups water
* 1 bunch of scallions, halved and cut into 2-3 inch lengths
* 1 tsp salt
* Oil for cooking

Preparation:

1. Mix all ingredients together and let sit for about 10 minutes. Check consistency before cooking—batter should be a little bit runnier than American pancake batter, so that the Pa Jun cooks quickly and evenly.
2. Heat a saute pan over medium heat and coat with a thin layer of oil.
3. Pour batter to fill pan in a thin layer (about 1/3 of your batter should fill a regular saute pan).
4. Cook for 3-4 minutes until set and golden brown on bottom.
5. Turn over with help of spatula or plate (or flip it in the air if you are good at that) and finish by cooking 1-2 more minutes, adding more oil if necessary.
6. Serve with soy or spicy dipping sauce1.

(Serves 4 as an appetizer or a side dish)

MARUYA (PHILIPPINES)

The snack or merienda which, while roughly corresponding to the American coffee break or English tea, is really rather different. At merienda time, usually four in the afternoon and sometimes also around ten in the morning, the average Filipino takes his traditional snack. Foods served at merienda can be almost anything. The typical merienda fares, however, are native delicacies made from glutinous rice and coconut. Maruya, banana fritters, are amongst the most popular snacks at merienda time.

Ingredients

* 1/2 cup flour
* 3/4 tsp. baking powder
* 1/4 tsp. salt
* 1 egg
* 1 cup milk
* 3 ripe saba (banana plantain), peeled and sliced lengthwise
* 2 cups vegetable oil
* flour, for dredging · sugar

Cooking Procedures:

1. In a bowl, sift together flour, baking powder and salt. Add milk and egg, beat until smooth.
2. Heat oil in a frying pan (or a large saucepan) over medium heat.
3. In batches, roll banana slices in flour and then dip in batter. Fry in hot oil until golden brown.
4. Drain on paper towels. Roll in sugar. Place in a serving dish and serve.

PISANG GORENG (INDONESIA)

Pisang Goreng (fried banana in Indonesian) is a snack food mostly found throughout Indonesia, Malaysia and Singapore. It is consumed as a snack in the morning and afternoon due to its warm nature in serving. In Indonesia, Pisang Goreng is often sold by street vendors, although some sellers have a storefront from which to sell their wares. Pisang Goreng Pontianak are widely popular in Indonesia and exclusively sold in certain retail outlets. The Banana is battered and then deep fried. The fritters that result are often sprinkled with a cinnamon sugar and occasionally served with fresh cream. Today's pisang goreng are more sophisticated and served in various ways, such as with cheese, jam, or chocolate.

Ingredients:

1 1/4 cups all-purpose flour
2 tablespoons granulated sugar
1/4 tablespoon vanilla powder
1/2 cup milk
1 egg
2 tablespoons butter, melted
4 ripe bananas, sliced
2 cups oil for frying

Directions:

1. In a large bowl, combine flour, sugar and vanilla powder. Make a well in the center, and pour in milk, egg and melted butter. Mix until smooth. Fold in banana slices until evenly coated.
2. Heat oil in a wok or deep-fryer to 375 degrees F (190 degrees C).
3. Drop banana mixture by tablespoon into hot oil. Fry until golden brown and crispy, 10 to 15 minutes. Remove bananas from oil, and drain on paper towels. Serve hot.

FALAFEL (MIDDLE EAST)

The popularity of this vegetarian fritter throughout Turkey, the Middle East and North Africa is not in doubt. Crisp to the point of crunch on the outside, tender and well—spiced within, the irresistible falafel are a rich source of protein. Falafel is very easy to make and with a little effort it would come out great. Falafel is served in a toasted bread, with some salads and spicy sauces. In Israel, as well as most of the Arab countries, they eat the falafel inside a pita bread, with vegetable salad and pickles.

Ingredients:

2 cups of dried chickpeas, soaked in water for 12 hours
Crumbs from 2 slices of white bread
5 cloves of garlic
2 teaspoon baking soda
1/3 cup chopped parsley
1/2 cup chopped coriander
1/2 small onion
1 spoon of sesame seeds
1 teaspoon cumin spice
1 teaspoon paprika
Salt, pepper.
Oil for deep frying

Method

Wash the soaked chickpeas and put them in a food processor with the garlic, onion and spices. Grind until you get a rough moist texture. Add a little water if needed.

Move the mixture into a large bowl, add the rest of the ingredients and put aside, covered, for 30-60 minutes. Add the baking soda to the mixture and knead a little. Wet your hands and shape little balls (smaller then apricots).

Warm the oil—it should be hot, not boiling. Fry until you get a deep brown shade. Serve hot!

SPINACH OMELET (EGYPT)

Egyptian cuisine's history goes back to Ancient Egypt. Archaeological excavations have found that workers on the Great Pyramids of Giza were paid in bread, beer, and onions, apparently their customary diet as peasants in the Egyptian countryside. Onions remain the primary vegetable for flavoring and nutrition in Egyptian food. Beans were also a primary source of protein for the mass of the Egyptian populace, as they remain today. Egyptian cuisine is notably conducive to vegetarian—and vegan diets, as it relies so heavily on vegetable dishes. Though food in Alexandria and the coasts of Egypt tends to use a great deal of fish and other seafood, for the most part Egyptian cuisine is based on foods that grow out of the ground. Meat has been very expensive for most Egyptians throughout history, and a great deal of vegetarian dishes have developed to work around this economic reality.

Ingredients

* 12 ounces fresh baby spinach
* 2 tablespoons canola or vegetable oil
* 2 medium onions, chopped
* 2 medium tomatoes, peeled and chopped
* salt
* fresh ground pepper
* 6 eggs
* ¼ teaspoon nutmeg
* 2 tablespoons canola or vegetable oil
* 1 (15 ounces) can chickpeas, rinsed and drained

Directions

1. Rinse and drain spinach; squeeze out excess water.
2. Place spinach in saucepan over medium heat; cover with lid and allow to wilt.
3. Remove from heat and drain in colander.
4. Remove all excess water.
5. Heat oil in large cast-iron skillet or other ovenproof skillet.
6. Add chopped onions and cook until tender and lightly golden.
7. Add tomatoes to skillet; season to taste with salt and pepper.
8. Cook for 12-15 minutes or until tomato is tender and liquid is reduced.
9. Preheat broiler.
10. Beat eggs lightly in bowl; season to taste with salt and pepper.
11. Add nutmeg to flavor the eggs, stirring well.
12. Add tomato mixture and spinach to beaten eggs and mix well.
13. Heat the remaining 2 tablespoons oil in cast-iron or ovenproof skillet; pour mixture in.
14. Top with canned Chickpeas.
15. Cook over low heat for approximately 10-12 minutes or until the bottom has set; then place under broiler to finish setting the top.
16. It should be firm and lightly browned when it is done.
17. Cut into slices and serve.

DOLMA (IRAN)

Iranian cuisine is often referred to as "Persian." This is because, until 1934, Iran was known as Persia. Curry (a spice) was adapted from the people of India and incorporated into the Persian (now Iranian) cuisine. Modern spicy curry stews demonstrate India's influence. The Indians also adapted foods from the Persians. A northern Indian cuisine called mughulai is modeled after what the Persians commonly ate. Dishes such as kofta (KOFtah, meatballs) and pilau (POO-lau) are now common to both Iranians and northern Indians. The idea of stuffing leaves, vines, fruits, and vegetables with various fillings was reinforced by the Turks. Dolma (Stuffed Grape Leaves) have become very popular throughout the Middle Eastern countries.

Ingredients

* 1 jar grape leaves (available at most Greek, Middle Eastern, and Italian markets)
* 1½ cups uncooked rice
* 1 medium onion, diced
* ¼ cup olive oil
* 2 cups water
* ½ cup fresh parsley, chopped
* 2 Tablespoons fresh dill, chopped
* 1 teaspoon fresh mint, chopped
* ¼ cup feta cheese, crumbled
* ½ cup pine nuts
* ½ cup raisins
* ½ cup lemon juice
* Salt and pepper, to taste

Procedure

1. In a saucepan, sauté the onion in olive oil until light brown.
2. Add rice and brown lightly.
3. Add the water, salt, and pepper.
4. Bring the water to a boil and simmer for 5 to 7 minutes, or until water is absorbed but rice is only partially cooked.
5. Make certain rice does not stick or burn.
6. Add all the ingredients except the lemon juice and mix well.
7. Drain the grape leaves and place 1 Tablespoon of filling in the center of each leaf.
8. Fold the sides in and roll the leaf up.
9. Place stuffed leaves in a pot in even and tight rows covering the bottom of the pan. When the bottom layer is complete, start another layer. Continue rolling dolmas until all of the filling is used.
10. Add ½ of the lemon juice and enough water to cover half of the rolled leaves.
11. Place a plate on the top layer to hold the stuffed leaves down and to prevent them from unrolling while cooking.
12. Simmer over low heat until most of the liquid is absorbed, about 45 minutes.
13. Remove the plate and dolmas from the pan, drizzle with olive oil and lemon juice, and serve. May be served warm or at room temperature. Serve with Yogurt and Mint Sauce

SOU BARAG (ARMENIA)

An Armenian delicacy, these cheese and phyllo turnovers are certain to be a big hit at your next cocktail party. Armenians make these for special occasions . . . and while they are somewhat labor intensive, the reward is in the finished product. Simply delicious!

Ingredients

* 1/2 lb Jack Cheese
* 3/4 lb Feta Cheese
* 1/2 cup Italian Parsley
* 2 eggs beaten
* salt and pepper to taste
* Mix well by hand.

***Note, to entertain larger parties, increase the quantity of ingredients in the aforementioned proportions.

Directions

1. Render one stick of unsalted butter. Reserve this for use shortly.
2. Using 4" wide sheets of phyllo dough (purchased at your local supermarket), butter the 'top facing' side of phyllo dough and place a reasonable portion of the prepared mixture onto the sheet at one end. Begin folding the phyllo dough corner to corner. You will use approximately one (4" wide) sheet of phyllo dough per barag.
3. Do this until all of the mixture has been used.
4. Place the triangles on a buttered cookie sheet and cook in a pre heated oven at 375 degrees for 20 minutes. Lower the heat to 300 degrees and bake another 15 minutes. Depending on what type of oven is used, you will want to pay attention to the color of the phyllo dough. You will know the barags are done when the dough turns golden brown in color.

LOSH KEBAB (ARMANIA)

Armenia, a part of the erstwhile Soviet Union, had been dominated by many nations, due to its strategic location. Among the greatest empires that once controlled Armenia, the most important were those of the Greeks, Romans, Arabs, Turks, Persians and Mongols. The Armenian cuisine has been influenced by these nations. Armenians use a great variety of ingredients in their traditional dishes. Fish, diverse types of meats and numerous sorts of fruits and vegetables, combined with also a great number of condiments, lead to the uniqueness of the Armenian cuisine, both in taste and in look. The Armenians appreciate very much the snacks. Lamb is an essential ingredient in this case. Losh Kebab (lamb-burger) is evidence of this fact.

Ingredients

* 1 lb. ground lamb

* fresh chopped parsley to taste
* 2 lg. onions, chopped
* 1 green bell pepper, diced fine
* 1/3 can tomato paste
* 1/4 tsp. allspice
* salt to taste
* pepper to taste
* 1/4 cup flour
* 2 tsp lemon juice

Directions

Gently mix everything together. You don't want to over-work the meat or it will be tough. Form into patties and grill or broil to desired doneness.

HALABI KEBAB (YEMEN)

Yemeni hospitality is typically Arab. These people are particularly fond of hot and spicy foods so prepare for chilies in your dish. A hot relish called zhoug is a hot combination of chilies and pepper combined with cardamom, caraway, fresh coriander and garlic, and is used as a bread dip. Breads of all kinds, shapes, sizes and flavors can be found in shops, restaurants, homes and even the street. A barley bread called malvj is a favorite. Meat including lamb, goat, chicken, and fish are served. However, so little is available that meat may be consumed only once a week or less. Halabi Kebab is considered an exotic dish.

Ingredients

2 1/2 lb ground meat
3 tb flour
1 tb oil
1 ts salt
1 ts pepper
1 tb zhoug*
3 tb oil
1 finely chopped onion sliced mushrooms chopped parsley
3 eggs

Instructions

Combine ground meat with flour, 1 tbsp oil, salt, pepper and zhoug. Form the meat mixture into a 10-inch loaf. Make a well the entire length of the loaf.

Heat 3 tbsp of oil in a skillet. Saute together the onions, mushrooms and parsley until the onions are golden. Place the mixture in the well of the loaf. Lightly beat the eggs and pour over the vegetables.

Preheat oven to 350 degrees.

Pat the sides of the loaf together to close up the well, and wrap in aluminum foil. Bake for 30 minutes. The loaf may be served either hot or cold.

*Zhoug: In a blender, puree enough chili peppers to measure 1 cup. Puree parsley and coriander together and blend well with the chili peppers. Add garlic, seasonings and olive oil. Again, blend well. Put the zhoug in a jar and keep it in the refrigerator. It will remain fresh for many months.

MANTI (UZBEKISTAN)

Manti (meat dumplings) is the most popular and favorite Uzbek dish. In the Fergana valley, Samarkand, Tashkent and Bukhara, Manti is one of the major components of the diet of the local population. In other places, it is prepared on special occasions. The dish is juicy, flavorful, scrumptious and completely depends on fresh ingredients. It does take about 4 hours to make, from starting the dough until you taste your first deliciously luscious manta (manti is plural of manta).

Ingredients

Filling:

> Lamb—500grams
> Lamb fat—50 grams (optional)
> Onions—4-6 medium
> Salt, freshly ground black pepper, cumin—to taste

Dough:

> All purpose white flour—400 g
> Water—1/2 cup
> Salt

Steps for the Dough:

1. Salt the water to be saltier than what you think is salty enough. Add the salted water to the flour and mix until the dough comes together.
2. When the dough comes together, separate it into 2 equal parts and let rest for about half an hour.

3. Kneed the dough until it's all soft and no more lumps are visible.
4. Roll it out to be very thin (not too thin, but thin enough to steam the meat mixture that will go inside, about 1/4 of an inch, or slightly less).
5. Cut the dough into about 3 inch squares. If the squares aren't exact, that's OK.

Steps for the meat:

1. Dice the meat into very small pieces, about 1/16th inch in size. Dice/Mince the fat too. None of that ground meat some recipes call for.
2. Dice/mince the onion to be in very small pieces, but don't use the grater or a food processor. You want pieces of onion, not just onion juice and pulp.
3. Season with salt, pepper, and cumin.
4. Mix all together. The fat gives the juice/moisture/flavor when the packets are steamed.

Steps for assembling:

1. Spoon the meat mixture into the center of the dough square.
2. Fold 2 opposite sides of the dough so they meet above the meat mixture.
3. Fold the other 2 sides just like in Step 2. Now you should have all sides folded up above the meat mixture and you have 4 corners.
4. Put your finger to one of the side and fold 2 corners so they meet.
5. Do the same Step 4 on the opposite side. The top should look like it has an "8" on the top.

To cook, place these assembled manti into a steamer. Fill the main pot with about 8-10 cups of water and boil. Let it boil for about 45 minutes, and manti should be all ready.

SHISH TAWOOK (SYRIA)

Shish Tawook is a chicken breasts kebab very popular in Syria, Lebanon and Turkey where the name originates. There are many different recipes on marinading the chicken but they all share an essential ingredient, yogurt. In Syria, Shish Tawook is always served with Toum, a delicious garlic sauce/dip that marries beautifully with all grilled chicken varieties. Shish Tawook is either served as a part of a barbecue platter with bread, mezze . . . etc. or, quite often, as a sandwich in a flat bread roll or a bun.

Ingredients

Chicken breast cubes 400g
Red onion
Red pepper

For the Marinade:

Yogurt 2tbsp
Vinegar 1tsp
Paprika 1tsp
Chili powder 1/2tsp
Garlic powder 1tsp
Black pepper 1/2tsp
Salt
Olive oil 2tbsp

Toum sauce:

Mayonnaise 4tbsp
Greek style yogurt 2tbsp
White wine vinegar 1tsp
Garlic 3-4 cloves, crushed
Lemon
Salt

Directions:

Mix all the marinade ingredients, add the chicken and ideally leave in the fridge for a couple of hours. Cut the red peppers and the red onion into 1 inch squares. You can use green peppers or mushrooms if you wish. Once the chicken is marinated start to put it on the skewers alternating between a pieces of vegetables and chicken.

If it is summer cook on a coal barbecue in the garden. Otherwise heat a griddle pan till very hot. Put the chicken skewers and don't turn till one side starts to char to give the beautiful barbecue flavor. Once one side is ready turn the skewers and put the pan in a 200C hot oven to finish cooking for around 12 minutes. You can cook it fully on the griddle pan if you wish but I find the meat becomes too dry this way.

Mix all the ingredients of the Toum sauce with Salt and lemon to taste.

Serve the Shish Tawook with Arabic bread, Toum, salad and whatever mezze you like. Or simply spread some of the Toum sauce on the Arabic flat bread, add pickles and tomatoes if you wish and roll. In Turkey they serve the Shish Tawook with white rice and salad.

SHWARMA SANDWICHES (JORDAN)

There is a marvelous range of snacks that are presented in the cuisine of Jordan. These snacks are quite exceptional in nature, they are quick and easy to make and are truly very wholesome. Most of the snacks are filled with meat and vegetables in the traditional manner. The greatest aspect of these delicious snacks is that they do not take up a lot of time in preparation and all you need are the right ingredients and a proper known method of preparing these highly mouth watering and healthy snacks.

From Jordan come these delicious rolled and grilled sandwiches made from Lamb, Chicken, and Middle Eastern Spices.

Ingredients

* 1/2 pound Lamb meat, cut into strips

* 1/2 teaspoon ground cardamom seeds
* 1/2 teaspoon ground cinnamon
* 1/2 teaspoon ground nutmeg
* 1/2 teaspoon ground black pepper
* 1/2 teaspoon ground Cayenne
* 1/2 teaspoon salt
* 3 cloves garlic, minced
* 1/2 Onion, minced
* 1 bay leaf
* 1/2 cup lemon juice
* 1/2 cup red wine vinegar
* 6 large sections pita bread
* 2 tomatoes, chopped

Directions

1. Place the meat in a bowl.
2. In another bowl, combine the spices, salt, garlic, Onion, bay leaf, lemon juice, and vinegar, stir well, and pour it over the meat.
3. Marinate in the refrigerator for at least 2 hours.
4. Drain the meat from the marinade and pat dry.
5. Grill the meat over a hot charcoal or gas fire until done, about 10 minutes, turning often.
6. Divide the meat into the pita bread sections, add tomatoes and serve.

BABA GANOUSH (LEBANON)

Lebanese appetizers (mezze) are a very important part of lebanese cuisine. Before dinner a large selection of appetizers in tiny dishes is set out for diners. Mezze may include vegetables, kibbeh balls, savory pastries, yogurt, cheese, and olives. Lebanese restaurants compete with each other on the number of mezze dishes they offer and may serve as many as seventy. Eggplant dip (baba ganoush) is a favorite throughout the Middle East, where the eggplant is usually cooked over an open flame, giving the pulp a smoky flavor. Baking it directly on your oven rack will give the eggplant a similar flavor. Baba Ganoush makes a great party dip.

Ingredients

* 1 large eggplant
* 2 cloves garlic, peeled and crushed
* 1 teaspoon salt
* Juice of 2 lemons, about 6 tablespoons
* 4 tablespoons tahini (ground sea-same seeds paste)
* 2 tablespoons water, more if needed
* 4 tablespoons chopped fresh parsley for garnish

Method

* Preheat oven to 400 degrees F.

* Wash eggplant. Remove stem. Prick eggplant several times with a fork. Place directly on oven rack and bake for 30 minutes, or until very soft. Carefully remove from oven and cool.

* When eggplant is cool enough to handle, peel off skin. (*) Mash it in a medium bowl with a potato masher, or place in a food processor and process until smooth but not liquid.

* In a small bowl, crush garlic into the salt with the back of a spoon. Beat in lemon juice, tahini, and water. Stir into mashed eggplant. If baba ganoush is too thick, add water 1 tablespoon at a time until mixture is a soft, creamy consistency.

* Divide mixture among four small plates or serve in one dish. Garnish with parsley. Serve Baba Ganoush with pieces of pita bread to scooping it up with.

BATATA BIL KIZBARA (LEBANON)

The Lebanese cuisine has very old and strong roots, surviving the catastrophes was an easy thing. Lebanon features a diverse cuisine, which has incorporated many cooking concepts from other countries, in time. The Middle Eastern cuisine features many cooking concepts that originate in Lebanon. Batata bil kizbara (Potato with Coriander) is probably the most popular street snack of Lebanon, which is also the easiest to make at home.

INGREDIENTS:

1 kg (32 oz) potatoes
2 cups vegetable oil (for frying)
4 cloves garlic, crushed with a pinch of salt
1 tspn salt (as desired)
½ tspn ground red pepper (as desired)
2 tbls finely chopped fresh coriander a dash of dried coriander

PREPARATION:

Wash fresh coriander, drain and put on a clean piece of cloth to dry for 5 minutes. Peel potatoes, wash and cut into small cubes, rewash and drain.

Fry potatoes in hot oil until golden-brown, put on absorbent paper.

Mix garlic with salt and fry till fragrant in hot oil for 5 minutes.

Add to it potatoes, a dash of dry coriander, and red pepper.

Stir well for 2 minutes. Stir in fresh coriander then remove from heat.

Serve hot.

THE CONTINENT OF
AUSTRALIA AND OCEANA

Australian cuisine, other than the indigenous climate and produce, has been derived from the tastes of immigrant settlers to Australia and the produce they have introduced to the continent. The British colonial period established a strong base of interest in Anglo-Celtic style recipes and methods. Subsequent waves of multicultural immigration, with a majority drawn from Asia and the Mediterranean region, and the strong, sophisticated food cultures these ethnic communities have brought with them influenced the development of Australian cuisine. Besides the culinary heritage of the Anglo-Celtic majority, the cuisines of China, Germany, Greece, Italy, Lebanon, Malaysia, Thailand, and Vietnam are not only popular, but have also left the greatest impact on Modern Australian cuisine. In recent times there are also substantial influences and culinary trends from American cuisine, French cuisine, Indian cuisine, Japanese cuisine, Moroccan cuisine and Spanish cuisine.

Fresh produce is readily available and thus used extensively, and the trend (urged by long-term government health initiatives) is towards low-salt, low-fat healthy cookery incorporating lean meat and lightly cooked, colorful, steamed or stir-fried vegetables. With most of the Australian population residing in coastal areas, fish and seafood is popular. In the temperate regions of Australia vegetables are traditionally eaten seasonally, especially in regional areas. During Spring: Artichoke, Asparagus, Beanshoots, Beetroot, Broccoli, Cabbage, Cauliflower, Cucumber, Leek, Lettuce, Mushrooms, Peas, Rhubarb, and Spinach. During Summer: Capsicum, Cucumber, Eggplant, Squash, Tomato, and Zucchini.

Australia's climate makes barbecues commonplace. Barbecue stalls selling sausages and fried onion on white bread with tomato or barbecue sauce are common in fund raising for schools or community groups. These stalls are called "Sausage Sizzles".

Australia's 11 million square kilometre fishing zone is the third largest in the world and allows for bountiful access to seafood which significantly influences Australian cuisine. Clean ocean environments around Australia produce high quality seafoods for domestic consumption and export.

As the majority of the populous live in capital cities relatively close to the sea, the cuisine of these regions has been influenced by involving quality fresh seafood. Filleted "ready to cook and eat" preparations are more popular as opposed to whole fish or any seafood product which contains bones.

MEAT PIE (AUSTRALIA)

The Australian diet has been heavily influenced by peoples from all over the world. The Potato Famine of the 1840s in Ireland led many desperate starving Irish people to leave their homeland, seeking relief in Australia. Gold was discovered in Australia a few years later, bringing more people to the country. Following World War II (1939-45), Europeans and Asians arrived in greater numbers. As a result, cuisines from other countries, such as Italy, Greece, and Lebanon, became popular. Meat pie, with dozens of recipe variations, is considered the Australian national dish.

Ingredients

* 2 pounds ground meat
* 1 cup ketchup
* 1 cup onion, chopped
* 1 teaspoon salt
* 1 cup milk
* ⅔ cup bread crumbs
* 1 teaspoon oregano
* ½ teaspoon pepper
* 2 Tablespoons Worcestershire sauce
* 2 cups cheddar cheese, shredded
* 2 prepared pie shells, 8-inch

Procedure

1. Preheat oven to 350°F.
2. Combine ground meat, ketchup, onion, salt, milk, breadcrumbs, oregano, and pepper in a bowl.
3. Mix well.

4. Divide mixture into 2 pie shells and bake for about 45 minutes.
5. While the pies are baking, mix together Worcestershire sauce and cheese in another bowl.
6. After about 45 minutes, remove pies from oven.
7. Spread Worcestershire sauce and cheese mixture on top of pie shells.
8. Bake for about 10 more minutes, or until cheese is melted.

DEVILED EGGS (NEW ZEALAND)

Snacks require just as much thought and balance as the other three main meals of the day. Snacks do have an important role to play in our diet. Healthy nutritious choices help ensure energize growth and activity. Basing snack choices around wholesome foods instead of processed food also provides a good source of vital nutrients. These basics on nutritious snacks no one knows better than Kiwi families, an example of which is their very popular, though simple, party snack—Deviled Eggs.

Ingredients:

* 6 hard-cooked eggs
* 1/4 cup minced scallions (green onions)
* 3 tablespoons mayonnaise
* 2 teaspoons Dijon mustard
* 1 teaspoon soy sauce
* 1 teaspoon chile paste with garlic
* 1/2 teaspoon sugar
Chopped scallions (green onions), for garnish
Salt and pepper to taste.

Preparation:

Shell the hard-cooked eggs and cut 1/4-inch off the ends of each one; reserve these trimmings. Halve the eggs crosswise, and remove the yolks. Set the whites aside. Place the yolks and the trimmings in a bowl. Add minced scallions, mayonnaise, Dijon mustard, soy sauce, chile paste, pepper, salt and sugar to the bowl. Mash with a fork until just smooth but not mushy. Spoon the mixture into the reserved egg whites, or pipe it in with a pastry tube. Sprinkle with the chopped scallions.

BANANA SCONES (FIJI ISLANDS)

Fijian food has a wonderful mix of the spicy curries that are influenced by the Indian people and the coconut, fish, sweet potato, cassava, bananas and other vegetables that the Fijians bring to the culture. Over time this food has developed and evolved to the current mix of flavors we experience now. Banana scones are a very popular snack for parties and school lunches.

Ingredients

* 2 cups flour
* 1/2 teaspoon salt
* 3 teaspoons baking powder
* 2 tablespoons butter, melted
* 1/4 cup mashed banana
* 1/4 cup sugar
* 1 egg
* 2 tablespoons

Directions

1. Sift flour, salt and baking powder together and out in bowl
2. Beat egg and combine with milk, melted butter, sugar and banana.
3. Stir the egg-banana mixture into a hollow in the middle of the flour. Mix the flour and banana with a fork.
4. When all the flour is mixed in, put table spoons of the scone mixture on a greased baking tray and bake in a hot oven till brown—about 15 minutes.

This mixture could also be made into fried scones or cooked on a greased roti iron.